Administrative Discretion in Action

Administrative Discretion in Action

A Narrative of Eminent Domain

Amanda M. Olejarski

LEXINGTON BOOKS
Lanham • Boulder • New York • Toronto • Plymouth, UK

Published by Lexington Books
A wholly owned subsidiary of The Rowman & Littlefield Publishing Group, Inc.
4501 Forbes Boulevard, Suite 200, Lanham, Maryland 20706
www.rowman.com

10 Thornbury Road, Plymouth PL6 7PP, United Kingdom

British Library Cataloguing in Publication Information Available

Library of Congress Cataloging-in-Publication Data Available

ISBN: 978-0-7391-7858-4 (cloth : alk. paper)
ISBN: 978-0-7391-7859-1 (electronic)

∞™ The paper used in this publication meets the minimum requirements of American National Standard for Information Sciences—Permanence of Paper for Printed Library Materials, ANSI/NISO Z39.48-1992.

To Ryan,
for everything

Contents

Tables and Figures

TABLES

FIGURES

Foreword

Charles T. Goodsell, Virginia Tech

Dr. Amanda M. Olejarski, assistant professor of public administration at Shippensburg University, has studied in concerted fashion the law, process and politics of eminent domain for more than seven years. She has presented many papers, published articles and lectured on the subject and wrote her dissertation at Virginia Tech on this topic. (Among the graduate students she was affectionately known as "SPED," a nickname she explains shortly.)

This is a highly informative volume for academics, specially in the field of public administration where the topic has been largely ignored. More importantly, the book will be a most useful practical guide for elected officials, public administrators, and citizens who get caught up in governmental "takings" of private property. Indeed the author refers to her book as a tool to inform and facilitate dialogue among people active inside and outside government on this sensitive matter. As such, it is written in a clear and direct style, largely in the nature of an informal narrative. Olejarski does not preach dogmatically, advocate one side or another, or pronounce final conclusions. Rather, she reviews the issue's legal history, provides factual information on its considerable complexities, and reminds us of the opposing values and heavy stakes involved.

Aside from wide examination of published legal and academic sources, the book is built on a foundation of field research. This was done in the state of Connecticut, in that it was here that the leading recent U.S. Supreme Court decision on the subject originated, *Kelo et al. v City of New London et al.*, handed down in 2005 (545 U.S. 469). Her suitably mixed-method research strategy includes a survey of local government officials in the state and in-depth interviews in the city of New London, the site of a taking that condemned valued neighborhood property for the purpose of allowing a private-public development corporation to enable the construction of a large plant by Pfizer, Inc. The author's special attention to this event allows her to go beyond a broad overview of the subject and penetrate it deeply at the human level.

The power to exercise eminent domain in the United States emanates from what seems like an almost throw-away phrase at the very end of the Constitution's lengthy Fifth Amendment, "nor shall private property be taken for public use, without just compensation." Over time, the inherent focus in these words on the adequacy of adequate monetary compensation has been largely supplanted by debate over what "public use" entails. Possibilities are the transfer of private property to ownership by government for its own activities (as in building a highway), serving the public good in general (e.g., removing slums), or making it possible for private developers to build and profit from business enterprises (like waterfront plazas and shopping malls). Because of the *Kelo* decision, determination of which or all of these options are permissible is turned over to the states. At present, forty-three state legislatures have passed statutes on the subject.

However, even these standards are often vague, no doubt because of the political sensitivity of the topic. As a result, individual local governments that encounter the issue have been forced to interpret the power's extent on their own. Hence local elected officials and administrators find themselves in the position of having to wend their way, alone, through the sticky legal and political wicket of how to attract new private investment to their revenue-starved jurisdictions while attempting to ride out the outcries of displaced homeowners and the loss of beloved neighborhood districts.

Olejarski's foremost theme in the book is to explore the normative and practical dimensions of the administrative discretion that local government practitioners must exercise in this volatile tinderbox. She points out that wise implementation involves not only mastering the technical details of negotiations, hearings and contracts, but grappling with politically powerful competing forces and working through distressing moral dilemmas. The very future of communities is at stake. Administrators must deal with the lobbying power of large corporations and their high-priced lawyers, the desperation of city councilpersons facing the need for a boost to their local economy, the personal hurt felt by residents whose private home and personal life are upended, and the political fallout from conservatives that champion private property rights and liberals who dislike using public authority to satisfy private investors.

In her close-up examination of what went on in New London, Olejarski brings her subject to life by describing in detail personal conversations in the kitchens of homeowners affected. Before-and-after photographs are provided of affected properties, including Ms. Kelo's now gone "Pink House" that spawned the litigation in the first place. In this exploration she discovers that a number of lapses in good judgment occurred in how administrative discretion was exercised.This includes not giving proper notice and failing to engage affected citizens in meaningful dialogue. In addition she learned that administrators who become involved in takings vary considerably in their knowledge of the process and their personal attitudes toward seizing citizen property. As a consequence, she recommends that they should exercise this august power only after talking with all the experienced professionals they can find, keep displaced citizens and the community at large honestly informed, and be proactive in discussing with their own elected officials what seems doable and right.

While the book's topic is a single policy area not commonly encountered in pubic administration as a whole, her study generates broad overall lessons for all conscientious public servants. She urges that while dealing with the particular problems and dilemmas of day-to-day administration, they should ponder the fundamental norms that must infect the running a constitutional democratic republic; leaven rational calculations with common sense; keep in mind the ideals of common fairness, public interest and public good; search continuously for more creative ways of doing things; deal with citizens with total integrity so as not to undermine public trust in government; remain open to hearing the interests and opinions of all parties; and seize the high ground by appropriately interpreting the law in light of their own best instincts and local circumstances.

Preface

My inspiration for this book occurred during the second week of my doctoral studies at the Center for Public Administration and Policy (CPAP) at Virginia Tech. What quickly became some of my most enjoyable memories were the times spent with colleagues outside of the Thomas Connor House in Blacksburg, where we would all gather during class intermissions. It was a break in the middle of John Rohr's institutional class, Normative Foundations of Public Administration (in which many of us learned to drink the CPAP kool-aid). A new friend, Chuck Kirby, asked me if I thought we were going to cover the *Kelo* case this semester, since the class was about ethics, and Rohr's *Ethics for Bureaucrats* centers around property as a regime value of Americans. I was only vaguely familiar with the case, having attended a lecture on "Hurricane *Kelo*" while working on my MPA at Rutgers, Camden. That afternoon, I went home, opened an academic search engine, typed in "eminent domain," and was absolutely stunned that only 161 articles had been written on the subject *ever*.

It was on that day that I decided to write my dissertation on eminent domain. The more investigating I did, the more amazed I became at how little the field of public administration had researched the subject. Certainly, the academic side of the field has made strides since then, but we are nowhere near catching up with the needs of our applied practitioners. I devoted every class paper to learning about takings. I was so proud when I earned the nickname SPED, specialist in eminent domain, from my classmates and professors.

Almost three years later, I found myself in New London, Connecticut, interviewing practitioners of public administration and community members about eminent domain. As an overly-eager graduate student, people were so gracious and willing to share candidly their knowledge and experiences with me. What I learned during that hot August week has been difficult to capture in words on a page.

So, what *is* eminent domain, and what does it mean when some gets "Kelo'd"? Eminent domain, also known as a *taking*, is the governmental power to take private property for public use, according to the Fifth Amendment of the U.S. Constitution. The landmark U.S. Supreme Court decision on eminent domain is the 2005 *Kelo v. New London* case. In *Kelo*, economic development was determined to meet the requirement for public use. In other words, increased tax revenue and job growth get the constitutional stamp of approval for the government to take private property. Now, this was not a new constitutional question. The Court ruled in the 1950s that economic development was a viable use for eminent domain. But *Kelo* was an outlier, an extreme case that continues to spark political controversy. Part of this controversy comes from the intertwining relationship between the local government and a pharmaceutial giant. Public perception is everything, and much of the public perceived *Kelo* as an abuse of eminent domain because it viewed the government taking property from one private party (homeowners) and giving it to another private party (Pfizer). This controversy was intensified by national media coverage of the taking, highlighting these perceived abuses of administrative power, hence, the narrative of eminent domain.

One of the most important lessons I learned at CPAP is about the importance of dialogue. As long as people keep talking, things *should* get better. And as I continued conducting interviews, I came to realize *that* was the problem with eminent domain: it has become such a controversial issue that practitioners and community members had stopped talking *to* one another and had begun speaking *past one another*.

That is why I wrote this book. This book should be used as a tool for interested practitioners, community members, scholars, and students: to facilitate dialogue during the governance process about using eminent domain responsibly. My understanding of governance surrounds the administration of public affairs in a political context. Especially important for a public administration book is the significance of administrative discretion, or the informal decision-making authority, sometimes called soft power, that practitioners exercise. This book, therefore, is also about critical reflection, analysis, and wielding administrative power, or about changing the way we *do* public administration. This book is about eminent domain in action.

In order to engage broadly those interested in issues surrounding eminent domain and administrative discretion in the academic and applied field of public administration, this is a deliberately short book written in an informal, more casual tone than many academic books. For this book to meet its goal of being used as a tool, I have emphasized praxis, or the dynamic, critical interface of theory and practice. I hope that its substantive practical value is balanced appropriately with theoretical considerations.

Acknowledgments

I would like to share my thanks to the faculty at the Center for Public Administration and Policy (CPAP) at Virginia Tech, Blacksburg, for their unwavering encouragement, guidance, and inspiration. I am especially grateful to Larkin Dudley, John Rohr, Gary Wamsley, Charles Goodsell, and Jesse Richardson for their mentoring of a young scholar. To my fellow CPAPers, for challenging me to succeed, for teasing me about my borderline obsession with eminent domain, and for providing moral support. Most deserving of gratitude is Kathy Webb Farley, my dear friend.

My thanks are also owed to Jim Garnett of Rutgers University, John Morris of Old Dominion University, and Cam Stivers of Cleveland State University, all of whom shared valuable insight to the conceptualization of this book. My new colleagues at Shippensburg University have provided incredible support, especially Alison Dagnes, Cynthia Botteron, and Sara Grove. Shippensburg public administration students Stefanie Pfister, Meagan Thorpe, and Tim Carr provided critical feedback and editorial assistance.

This book could not have been written without the time and contributions of the many practitioners and community members with whom I spoke. I am keeping administrators' names confidential but need to extend my sincere appreciation to them. Community members Amy Visciglia, Kathleen Mitchell, Susette Kelo, Timmy LeBlanc, Avner Gregory, June Evered, and Doug Schwartz—thank you for opening your homes to me and sharing your stories.

Finally, my husband, Ryan, to whom this book is dedicated—for being more supportive than I sometimes deserve and for keeping our fur babies and me happy.

Part I

PRESENTING THE PROBLEM

Part I introduces readers to a significantly overlooked problem for practitioners of public administration: the responsible management of the power of eminent domain. Administrators' should acknowledge the power they wield via discretion in the governance process. The normative-constitutionalist approach throughout this book facilitates an exploration of the discretion exercised in the decision-making process of eminent domain.

Chapter One

Eminent Domain in Action

Nor shall private property be taken for public use, without just compensation.

—Takings Clause, Fifth Amendment, United States Constitution

Most people are probably familiar enough with "the little blue pill," Pfizer's miracle drug that was introduced during the late 1990s. What could that possibly have to do with public administration? The little blue pill was at the center of a national battle over private property rights that began during the summer of 1996 in a small Connecticut community and ended at the United States Supreme Court in June of 2005 with *Kelo v. New London.*

We all know that saying, "This would be funny if. . . ." Well, the fact that the little blue pill made it to the highest court in America would be funny if . . . it weren't true. It would also be funny if it weren't true that a $1,350 bill made it to the Supreme Court . . . and that Congress passed a law condemning a neighborhood that was almost 98 percent black in the middle of the civil rights movement, which made it to the Supreme Court . . . and that a state law allowing renters to have homes condemned so they could purchase them (with a state loan of 90 percent) because the Dole fruit company owned too much property also made it to the Supreme Court.

All of these cases are true, and all of these cases have to do with eminent domain. In what would later become more of a Pyrrhic victory, the Supreme Court settled the immediate controversy of the 2005 *Kelo* eminent domain case, resulting in state legislatures rushing to pass laws at the invitation of the highest court in the land. Enter public administrators in municipalities and states across America. . . .

Eminent domain, also known as a taking, is the governmental power to take private property for public use. The takings power is enumerated, or expressly granted, in the Fifth Amendment of the United States Constitution. The *Law & Order* effect on constitutional principles has resulted in the public's heightened familiarity with the other rights and powers outlined in the amendment, such as "pleading the fifth," double jeopardy, and, of course, the right to due process. Often overlooked, however, is the last line: "Nor shall private property be taken for public use, without just compensation." This is known as the Takings Clause.

What is most important for public administrators is that the Takings Clause inherently pits two high-stakes rights in direct opposition to one another: the private property rights of individual citizens and the governmental right to advance the public good via eminent domain. Here is what makes this book a public administration book: this fundamental conundrum is the foundation of the balancing act that practitioners endure in the decision-making process. It is this dynamic interface that presents the opportunity for administrators to exercise their discretion, or informal authority. Simply put, administrative discretion is the power to interpret, to understand, and to implement vague laws and policies. Here, the focus is on practitioners' use of discretion in the context of eminent domain.

Often characterized as dichotomous, this relationship between private property rights and the public good assumes a significant role in the governance process. It creates an environment in which practitioners of public administration must strike a balance between these two significant rights when making decisions surrounding takings issues. But these decisions should not be made in a vacuum. Public administrators should involve community members in the process. The difficulty in doing this the central premise of this book: that practitioners and government officials should engage in dialogue with the community but that the two groups are usually talking past one another, unable to engage with one another. Hence, the normatively-based approach of this book, an approach inclusive of values (in addition to empirical facts), or the way decisions *should* be made.

The impetus for this book is the widespread public reaction to the most recent eminent domain case, *Kelo v. New London*, in 2005. Its universality results from the foundational ideas surrounding dialogue during the takings process. What makes this book unique is the ability to educate by providing both perspectives, government officials and community members actually involved with eminent domain, in the hopes of helping both sides engage in dialogue with one another. Incorporating a narrative-style here facilitates an appreciation for the human side of governance and policy implementation.

Critical reflection and analysis of this kind helps us to change the way we think about and conduct public administration.

PROBLEM OF EMINENT DOMAIN

This balancing act of two public goods came to a boiling point in the summer of 2005 with the Supreme Court's landmark decision in *Kelo v. New London.*[1] Here, the highest court in the land was divided five to four in favor of allowing eminent domain to be used for some degree of private benefit in the name of economic redevelopment. More will be discussed on the decision later, but it is sufficient to note that *Kelo* brought these issues of private property rights and the governmental takings power to the forefront of public debate. The lack of agreement, signified by the 5-4 decision, within the Court highlights the controversial nature of eminent domain.

In the ruling, the Court explicitly stated that nothing in their ruling prohibited any state from enacting revised takings legislation. The states took this as their personal, engraved invitation, and since the 2005 ruling, forty-three states have RSVP'd.[2] This presents the problem of eminent domain: Now that the Court has deferred to state legislatures, which have passed takings legislation in what may best be described as a flurry of legislative activity, practitioners of public administration have the responsibility of implementing eminent domain policies. During this implementation process, administrators exercise their discretion in making decisions.

Post-*Kelo* takings statutes are frequently vague and use conflicting language.[3] This duality of deference, in that the Court defers to state legislatures, which then defer to practitioners, results in fertile ground for the study of administrators actually involved in the interpretation and implementation of eminent domain policies. And that is the purpose of this book: to educate interested individuals in the field by gaining a better understanding of how public administrators and community members understand eminent domain. While a seriously neglected arena of study, eminent domain presents a dynamic case study to provide context to explore administrators' use of discretion. *Kelo* is an excellent example for public administration to study because of its sweeping public controversy and familiarity, as well as all the nuance it provides for critical analysis.

Exploring understanding and search for takings guidance involves focusing on the administrative discretion that practitioners possess when making decisions on issues relating to eminent domain. This is particularly important because of the inherently ambiguous nature of public policy and the power administrators' wield in implementing post-*Kelo* takings policies. Understanding this dynamic necessitates a consideration of the takings process with regard to the steps involved in initiating eminent domain, as well as the practitioners involved and the governance structure. All of this is *practically* significant because it provides context to decisions surrounding eminent domain that practitioners across the country face. It also allows us to see the complexity of the process and just how many people are involved, thus suitable for the *theoretical* study of discretion.

This book uses *Kelo* as a teaching tool to understand administrative discretion and governmental and community perspectives on eminent domain.[4] I conducted twenty-six interviews for this book: Nineteen public administrators throughout the state of Connecticut and seven community members directly involved with the *Kelo* case. To better prepare myself for the interviews, I conducted a small survey of 142 practitioners, also in Connecticut.[5] Studying the state most likely to have a grasp on the case, and, in turn, eminent domain, lends insight into administrators' understanding because they are in the most knowledgeable position to perceive and interpret relevant issues. This served a number of purposes, including ensuring that the "right" questions were asked of the "right" people during the interviews. In other words, the survey was designed to facilitate analysis of data to inform better the interview process, as well as to allow interested survey respondents to volunteer to participate in the interviews.[6]

ADMINISTRATIVE STRUCTURE OF CONNECTICUT GOVERNMENT

"Too many cooks in the kitchen," goes the saying, "spoils the recipe." In the case of eminent domain, there are *a lot* of cooks in the kitchen. Local governments have an executive chef (the administrative/executive branch), a sous chef (the legislative branch), and lots of prep cooks (the boards and commissions). To keep the analogy going, community members are the "patrons" of the restaurant, and grassroots organizers are the busboys and hostesses, responsible for much of the heavy lifting.[7]

Having so many cooks in the kitchen, cooking up plans involving eminent domain, is designed to help ensure that a transparent, deliberative decision-making process occurs (as shown in Figure 1.1). But the actual outcome is not always what was intended, which happened in *Kelo*. Sometimes, too many cooks *do* spoil the recipe, or the municipal plan for development that may involve the use of eminent domain. It is important to discuss how Connecticut government is organized to provide context on the responsibilities, constraints, and resources, for further discussions on the process of eminent domain, and what went wrong in *Kelo*.

Connecticut's administrative, or governance, structure differs from many other states in that there is no county level of government. Counties do exist for geographic boundaries, but they do not possess governmental authority over the state's 169 municipalities. Even more interesting, Connecticut municipalities have five different forms of local government in terms of the relationship between administrative and legislative bodies: Board of Selectmen-Town Meeting (103 localities), Manager-Council (30 localities), Mayor-Council (24 localities), Board of Selectman-Representative Town Meeting (RTM) (5 localities), and Mayor-Board of Aldermen (4 localities).[8] These will all be explained to show the relationships between the administrative and legislative branches of local government, and also the role of specialized boards and commissions. Think of this like the separation of powers and checks and balances we all learned about in Government 101 classes in college.

In the Board of Selectmen-Town Meeting form of government, the board, typically three members and led by a First Selectman, serves in an administrative capacity and is responsible for carrying out the locality's policies and ordinances. Legislative power rests with the Town Meeting, which is comprised of all registered voters in the municipality who are able to vote on issues during town meetings. The Board of Selectmen-Representative Town Meeting (RTM) form of government only differs in that RTM members are elected to represent members of the municipality's districts because of the larger population.

The Manager-Council form of government elects a City or Town Council of varying size, dependent on the population, which then appoints the City or Town Manager. Administrative responsibilities, such as enforcing local laws and ordinances, fall under the purview of the Manager; legislative activities are the responsibility of the Council. Under the Mayor-Council form, the Mayor acts as the administrative or executive for the municipality, with the Council fulfilling legislative duties as the governing body. The Mayor-Board of Aldermen government style functions similarly, with the Mayor as executive and the Board of Aldermen as legislative body.

Within these five forms of municipal government, however, exists subtle differences that add to the complexity of local government. While a municipality may employ a Manager-Council form of government, there may also be a Mayor to assume ceremonial responsibilities or to chair the Council meetings. Some localities may opt to include a Deputy Mayor or have a Chairman of the Council.

Various boards, commissions, and committees also assume a strong role in Connecticut municipal government. The authority of these organizations depends according to the locality, but some do possess decision-making authority, while others are advisory in nature. Fairly standard organizations in the governance structure include: Boards of Education, Finance, and appeals for Zoning and Assessments; Commissions of Planning, Zoning, Parks and Recreation. Also present are a number of social services commissions for youth and the elderly and committees, which are generally tailored to a municipality's particular needs, such as school buildings, community development, etc.

Since counties do not possess authority over local governments in Connecticut, there are judicial districts. These districts divide the state geographically for trial-court purposes. In Connecticut, there are thirteen judicial districts. Trial court, or the Superior Court, hears cases divided among civil, criminal, family, and juvenile issues. In *Kelo*, the judicial district was responsible for signing condemnation papers allowing the local government to take the private property via eminent domain.

PROCESS OF EMINENT DOMAIN

Eminent domain is the end result of a long, deliberative process. Eminent domain begins with an idea, a plan is developed by the local government, and then the plan is implemented. The process is also designed to be transparent, with the local government holding public hearings for community members and grass roots organizations to voice their perspectives. During my interviews, I asked administrators to describe the process in their locality. The following description is a result of their responses. Most important to note is that the eminent domain process outlined below is *ideal*, meaning it is the way the process *should* be done. But this is not always the case, like in *Kelo*.

First and foremost, the process of eminent domain begins with an idea. Ideas can come from anywhere, career civil servants, elected officials, citizens within the community, or even a private development corporation. Ideas may be based on needs, like road widening or school construction, or wants, such as parks and recreational facilities. But the process begins with an idea to redefine the community in some way, presumably for the betterment of society.

More logistically, a development project that could potentially involve the use of eminent domain is generally initiated by a local department, such as Public Works or Engineering; a commission, perhaps Land use Planning or school Building; an agency like Development or Redevelopment; or, in some instances, a private developer. The department, commission, agency, or developer that initiates the project consults with the relevant land use commissions in the locality to facilitate a thorough review of the project. Once the plan has been developed, it is further reviewed by additional boards and commissions, like the Zoning Commission and the Zoning Board of Appeals. This helps to ensure that eminent domain is avoided at all costs if possible. Most important during this stage of the process is ensuring that what land the plan requires includes a "reasonable use of the property," according to a zoning board of appeals chairman.

Here, the development plan is adjusted and re-tooled to identify alternative land when feasible to avoid using eminent domain if there are other properties available. These alternatives may emerge if the municipality currently owns property in another suitable location or if fewer residential properties may be taken in a different area. Zoning then grants permits to allow development on the proposed land or approves what are called variances, which allow changes to the zoning requirements on a particular property. Essentially, this process allows that which was previously considered an illegal use of the property to be permitted due to the particular circumstances of the development plan. An example is that land may be re-zoned to move the plan to an alternative location to preserve the initial parcels of land identified by the plan.

After the development plan has been reviewed by all relevant stakeholders, open community hearings are held to "educate and inform," in the words of one administrator, the public about the proposed project. Then, after public discussion, the administrative body of the locality authorizes the acquisition of the property needed for the development plan. This is done in consultation with the municipal attorney or an external legal firm contracted by the city, as well as what is typically an external real estate appraiser to appraise the value of the properties needed to be taken for the project. Again, there are more public hearings to discuss the value of properties necessary for the implementation of the development plan.

What follows is the authorization by the legislative body of the locality to acquire the property via eminent domain. Once again, representatives in the legislative body consult with the attorney and appraiser regarding the valuation of the properties. Though largely dependent upon local ordinances, authorization of property acquisition may involve a referendum on which the public would vote. For example, in one Connecticut municipality, any funding requests over one percent of the total budget must be approved by referendum; anything below that threshold may be approved by the municipal authorities. At this stage in the takings process, the Board of Finance holds additional public hearings and consults with the legislative body and the relevant land use commissions regarding funding the property acquisition.

Depending on local ordinances, final approval rests with either the legislative or the administrative body of the municipality. Administrators who participated in this study responded about equally in terms of whether final approval was under the purview of the legislative or administrative body. According to a zoning board of appeals chairman, the legislative body is unlikely to grant final approval without the support of the land use commissions.

Before final approval is granted, however, is the time during which precondemnation negotiations and other strategies are employed to avoid having to initiate official eminent domain proceedings. If these efforts fail to be successful, condemnation by the local government's power of eminent domain is the result. Generally, the attorney is predominantly involved in the negotiation process and is frequently accompanied by members of the administrative body or commission members.

When all else fails and eminent domain must be used for property acquisition, the judicial district (similar to county-level government in other states) becomes involved in the process. The chief clerk of the judicial district is responsible for signing a certificate of taking to acquire the property, according to one such retired administrator. The chief clerk who participated in this study continued to explain that the title to the property is then turned over to the locality.

The property owner may appeal the compensation of the taking but not the taking itself. According to administrators participating in these interviews, Connecticut state statutes are somewhat unusual in this regard. When asked to elaborate on why the state limits property owners' appeals to issues surrounding the compensation of a taking, a deputy chief clerk explained, "Because initially the Connecticut legislature decided that taking private property for public use was important enough to not give that option to a property owner." The chief clerk then continued, "Nobody ever raised that issue because it was probably never considered. . . . This [the *Kelo* case] was very unusual. Ninety-nine percent of the cases were clearly for public use."

Figure 1.1 provides a visual depiction of the takings process, as explained by administrators who were interviewed for this study. Administrators who participated in the survey and interviews for this book are a reflection of the roles and departments involved in the process of eminent domain.[9] Given my emphasis on understanding the interactions, relationships, and dynamics, or the administrative discretion, my definition of "administrators" is broad: I include career civil servants, appointed administrators, and elected officials. I did not include administrators without foreseeable decision-making authority; administrators without the formal authority to make decisions also inherently lack the informal authority, the discretion, to make important decisions. I did include, however, practitioners who were in supervisory and subordinate positions to account for formal and informal authority (discretion).

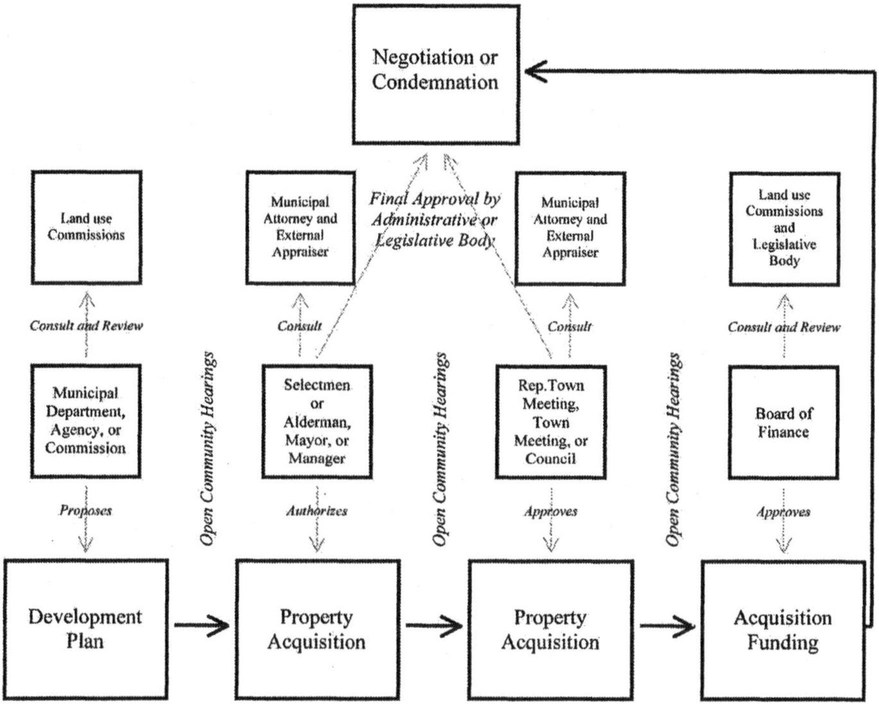

Figure 1.1 Eminent Domain Process

A NOTE ABOUT THE SURVEY AND INTERVIEW PARTICIPANTS

Discussion about the context of this book would be incomplete, however, without further details about the character and spirit of the administrators and community members who participated in this research. This is, after all, a narrative of eminent domain. When the survey was first deployed, I received numerous emails from administrators offering recommendations for books, other eminent domain cases, and websites to review, as well as countless well-wishes for a successful research project. In the midst of what can only be described as "dissertation-gate" (i.e., a catastrophic server configuration error with the listserv), administrators still continued to be supportive of my project, even completing the survey and volunteering to participate in an interview while receiving dozens of emails back and forth.

During the process of scheduling interviews, administrators were incredibly flexible with their time, which contributed to my ability to interview every single administrator who responded to my request. Even rush-hour traffic on Interstate 95, family emergencies, and unplanned vacations did not derail the interviews. To say that these administrators were flexible and supportive hardly seems to do justice to their kindness. Administrators who participated in the interviews were extremely forthcoming and spoke openly. They were generally very knowledgeable about takings and related issues and were able to provide specific examples of issues relating to eminent domain within and beyond their locality. Going beyond providing thicker description to the small survey, the interviews provided substantial insight into administrators' understanding and search for guidance during the implementation of eminent domain. More specifically, the interviews extended to factors contributing to understanding and guidance, political and legal authority to employ eminent domain, the role of public support in development projects, and facilitating a better understanding of the process of eminent domain. All of this contributes to the development and exercising of administrative discretion.

A last-minute addition to the interview consent form allowed administrators to be identified by name in publications if they chose. I made this alteration in the hopes of interviewing some of the key people involved in *Kelo*. Most administrators agreed to provide their names because it would "help me out," as one representative town meeting official said. One administrator drove me to visit the Long Island Sound during our interview, another kept me company on the phone for almost an hour while I sat in traffic, and a number of them offered to feed my caffeine habit. Others brought additional administrators into the interview with whom they thought I would be interested in speaking. One representative town meeting official even volunteered to take me on a tour of the Fort Trumbull neighborhood. One judicial district official even gave me the home address of the two community grassroots opposition leaders who spear-headed efforts against the takings in *Kelo*, therefore enabling me to understand the community members' perspectives I was so desperately seeking.

The efforts of these last two administrators helped to inform my research, beyond the scope of this research, in ways I could not have imagined. As I headed to New London, CT, for my tour of the *Kelo* site, I arrived much earlier than planned. Perhaps it was the temperature going to my head (it was the hottest week Connecticut had seen in years), but I decided to knock on the door of the grassroots opposition leaders. Amy Visciglia opened the door and said, "I heard about you, come on in." I had been communicating via email with Kathleen Mitchell, self-described on Facebook as "gadfly" and speechwriter for Susette Kelo. She let Amy and her husband, Steve, know that I was coming.

Amy and I spoke for over ninety minutes when I realized that I was late to meet June Evered for my tour of the neighborhood. She invited me to come back later that evening to finish. When I arrived, after briefly speaking with her and her husband, she put me on the phone with Kathleen, who then told me to come over—and to bring coffee filters! At the risk of making a long story that much longer, suffice it to say that I spent four very informative hours on Kathleen's front porch chatting with her; Susette Kelo; Susette's husband, Timmy LeBlanc; and Doug Schwartz, the mailman during the ten-year battle.

Earlier in the day, during my tour of the area, June and I went to visit the famous "little pink house," which has since been relocated to another lot in the city (ironically around the corner from the courthouse in which the condemnation paperwork was signed to authorize the taking of the *Kelo* properties). I had the good fortune to be there just as Avner Gregory, the man who owned the lot and paid to have the house relocated, arrived home. He invited us in, told the story of how the house came to be relocated, and even gave me a piece of the original little pink house that has come to symbolize eminent domain. One of my most cherished possessions, this piece of the little pink house is proudly placed in my office, next to the broken champagne flute from my dissertation defense and a signed copy of the famous (it received nation-wide publicity) Christmas card that Susette Kelo sent to all involved in *Kelo*, including *Supreme Court justices*. Written by New London grassroots activist Kathleen Mitchell, the card reads:

Here is my house that you did take
From me to you, this spell I make
Your houses, your homes
Your family, your friends
May they live in misery
That never ends.
I curse you all
May you rot in hell
To each of you
I send this spell
For the rest of your lives
I wish you ill
I send this now
By power of will

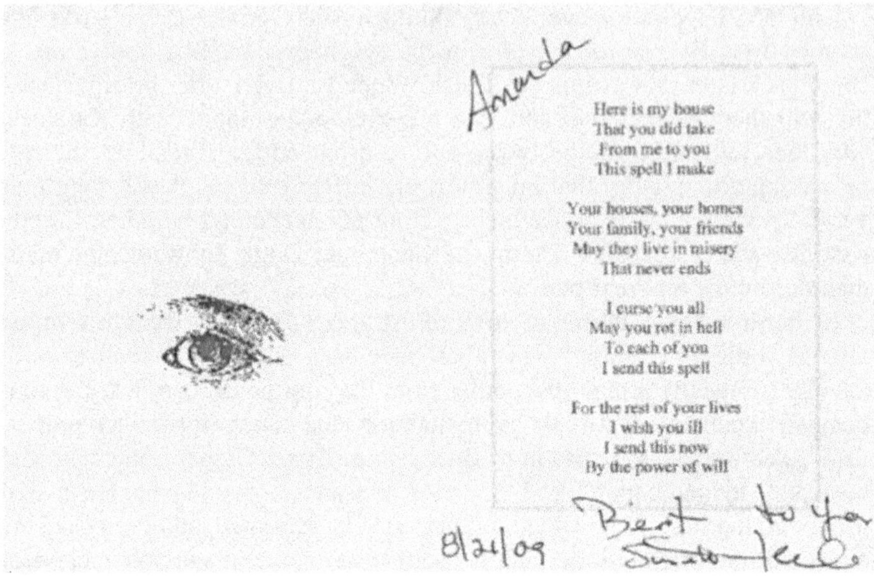

As Avner explained during our interview, there were three requirements to which he had to agree in order to have the little pink house relocated: that the house remain pink (a requirement with which he was less than thrilled because he lives in the home for six months out of the year, when he is not doing philanthropic work in India), that the house remain on the site for ninety-nine years, and that there be a plaque in front of the house to identify it as the "Kelo" house.

This plaque, which was dedicated on June 21, 2008, reads:

> This little pink house was the subject of the landmark 2005 US Supreme Court case *Kelo v. City of New London*, one of the most widely despised decisions in the Court's history. In *Kelo*, the Court ruled that New London could take this home and others and give the land to a private developer in the name of "economic development." The case caused a nationwide backlash against eminent domain abuse, resulting in reform legislation in more than 40 states and numerous state court decisions in favor of property owners. It also inspired increased citizen activism to protect property rights from takings for private development. This house, moved from the Fort Trumbull neighborhood, stands as a testament to the bravery of Susette Kelo and her neighbors, and to the thousands of others who have battled and are battling the abuse of eminent domain across the country.

Image 1.3. Plaque outside the little pink house in its new location at 36 Franklin Street in New London, CT. Source: Photo by the Author.

Image 1.4. Address marker outside the little pink house. Source: Photo by the author.

Image 1.5. The Kelo House. Source: Photo by the author.

NOTES

1. *Kelo et al. v. City of New London et al.* (545 U.S. 469 [2005]).
2. Castle Coalition (2009).
3. Olejarski (2011b).
4. In response to calls from the academic side of public administration to conduct mixed-method research (involving survey and interview analysis) with a practical emphasis, including the Minnowbrook III meeting (O'Leary, Van Slyke, & Kim 2011) and Riccucci's (2010) recent urging, the research design of this book uses what Cresswell & Clark (2010) call exploratory convergent parallel research design, which combines quantitative survey analysis with qualitative interview analysis.
5. Administrators' email addresses were collected from municipal websites listed on the Connecticut state website (www.ct.gov) and the directory of judicial district staff. See Appendix A for a complete listing on demographic characteristics of study participants, including local government departments in which participants are employed. The survey was open for three weeks during the summer of 2009. The total number of targeted administrators who received the survey was 2,125, which includes employees in 153 of 169 municipalities (those with working websites) and thirteen of thirteen judicial districts. A university listserv was set up to manage survey deployment. The response rate of the survey was 6.68 percent, or 142 public administrators. The goal of this survey was *breadth*; the survey response *rate* is small, however, the *number* of survey respondents (142) and *coverage of departments included* that are involved with eminent domain (shown in Appendix A) provides a comprehensive narrative of the takings process. See, for an example of *depth*, a 2010 journal article appearing in *Public Administration Review* by Hoyman and McCall in which they surveyed seventy-two North Carolina county managers on their attitudes toward eminent domain. See Appendix C for the complete survey instrument.
6. Of the 142 survey respondents, seventeen public administrators, or 11.97 percent, participated in an interview. The snowballing technique was also used to include two additional administrators, for a total of nineteen in-depth, semi-formal, elite interviews. Most interviews took place at the participant's location of convenience; four were conducted over the phone to accommodate vacation schedules. Interviews were recorded to allow for a more conversational flow, key to the elite interviewing technique. Interviews typically lasted between sixty and ninety minutes. All interviews took place in August 2009.
7. I should mention that I waited tables through most of college and graduate school, and my first official job with a Ph.D. was as a server.
8. Data collected from the Connecticut Economic Resource Center, Inc.'s "Town Profiles" (2009); three municipal governments have another form of government.
9. See Appendix A for complete demographic information on research participants.

Chapter Two

An "Eminent" Problem for Public Administration

> *The notion of praxis implies that as we acquire knowledge about our circumstances and as we view that knowledge in a critical manner, we are compelled to pursue more effective communication and greater autonomy and responsibility.*
>
> —Robert B. Denhardt, *Theories of public organization*[1]

In the last chapter, I wrote that the purpose of the book was to help educate government officials, future public administrators, and community members about both sides' perspectives and understanding of eminent domain in order to facilitate productive, transparent dialogue. But the goal is related to something called praxis: in public administration through the context of eminent domain. Praxis is more than a simple theory used to explore administrative behavior. Praxis is the relationship between theory and practice. It looks something like this: Theory → Practice, in which the arrow between the two is praxis, see Figure 2.1 below.[2]

Praxis is a way of thinking, a way of changing the ways in which we think about public administration. It should be critical and reflexive. A good starting point is Denhardt: "The notion of praxis implies that as we acquire knowledge about our circumstances and as we view that knowledge in a critical manner, we are compelled to pursue more effective communication and greater autonomy and responsibility."[3]

In other words, praxis necessitates understanding how we think about public administration in a critical and reflexive manner (theory) *before* we attempt to apply what we *think* we know (practice). The theory side of the equation involves considering our ontological and epistemological foundations; the assumptions, perspectives, and biases that color our ways of thinking; and the ways in which theories fit into broader contexts of frameworks, which, in

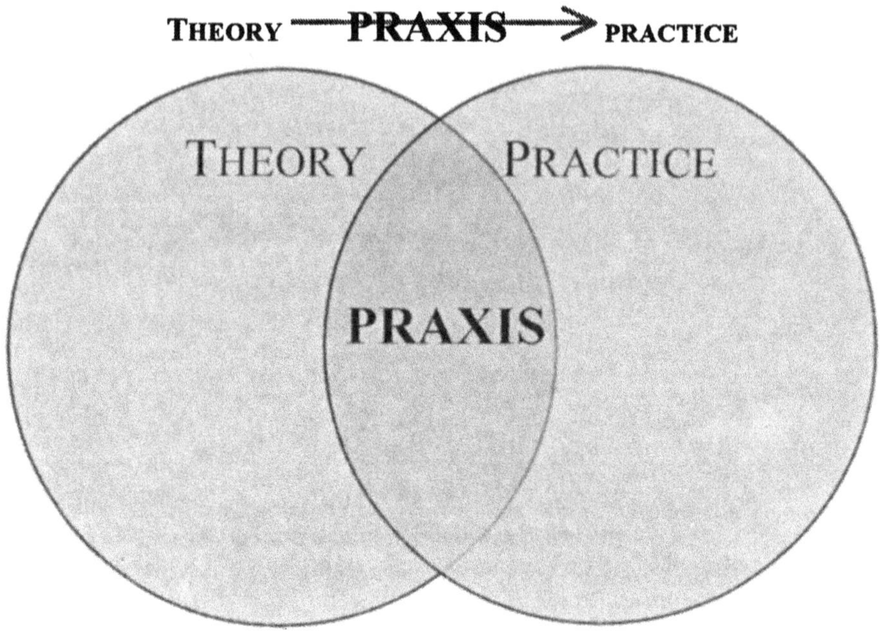

Figure 2.1. Praxis

turn, result in paradigms. At the other side of the equation is practice, or the applied side of the field of public administration. For example, the Takings Clause includes a requirement that eminent domain be used for *public use*, yet practice shows that public use has been expanded by the Supreme Court to a much broader *public purpose*. Praxis should be the interface between what theory tells us *should* happen, compared with what *does* happen in practice. This book's critical analysis of administrative discretion in the context of eminent domain is an example of praxis.

Here, we should consider the administrative amoeba, also known to some descendants of the Refounding Movement as the donut conundrum. Public administration is an all-encompassing field, pulling from countless disciplines, such as political science, economics, sociology, psychology, business, etc. Students of the field, whether practitioners or academics, should be mindful of the hierarchical and horizontal sharing of overlapping powers in our constitutional republic. It is through this top-down, bottom-up, left-right, and back again environment that the amoeba appears; readers would be hard-pressed to find a topic of study or current event that did not somehow relate to public administration. Without a heightened awareness of these broad considerations, we are subject to missing out on the donut, only being left with *a hole*.

Applying the idea of praxis to this book, the focus of study is on the relationships between administrative professionalism, or knowledge and experience, (theory) in the implementation of eminent domain (practice). In this equation, praxis manifests as administrators' discretion in action, or wielding administrative power. These relationships between professionalism and implementation, in light of discretion, are inherently grounded on normative foundations, or the way things *ought* to be. Therefore, the next sections will cover academic research: the reading may be a bit on the heavy side, but it is important to understand what administration discretion *really* means in order to understand how practitioners *really* exercise it when making eminent domain-related decisions.[4] This involves discretion, professionalism, the implementation of a legal case, public service motivation, relationships between politics and administration, public good and public interest, and governance. Exciting, I know, hold on to your thinking caps.

ADMINISTRATIVE DISCRETION

Administrative discretion involves practitioners using informal authority, or their ability to interpret policies, laws, and statutes. They exercise this discretionary authority when they decide what a policy means in the context of the decision they are trying to make. Discretion may also be described as soft power. For example, in *Kelo*, administrators used their discretion to determine that "public use" meant they could use eminent domain to take private property to build parks and roads and also office and retail space (more on this in chapter 3). *How* they came to this conclusion is part of what this book tries to study: their use of administrative discretion.

Theoretically, administrative discretion is practitioners' using their values, ethics, and morals, which they *should* hone from their professional development and training, expertise and competency, education, and experience. Practically, administrators *should* exercise their discretion in a way that is a reflection of the values of the community they serve, by being responsive to the public interest, that is balanced with their ability to use their expertise and professionalism, by being responsible in their decision-making.

In the context of eminent domain, discretion involves the power that administrators wield when they implement takings policies. Discretion is a *process*.[5] Administrators' discretionary activity surrounds their responsibility to "advise, report, respond, initiate, inform, question, caution, complain, applaud, encourage, rebuke, promote, retard, and mediate."[6] Practitioners, therefore, govern and participate in the policy-making process through all of these actions: by using discretion to determine how to implement a vague policy ("public use," for example), administrators are *making* policy. These decisions are not made in a vacuum. Discretion is influenced by internal and external pressures, such as those of the political and legal nature, and are constantly shifting.[7]

By making policy via exercising discretion, administrators use this power to overcome misconceptions about their executive and legislative roles. In other words, practitioners have an obligation to speak truth to power and acknowledge, first to themselves, that they *do* participate in policy-making.[8] Consider this from a separation of powers standpoint and the perspective that administrators exercise legislative power (when they use discretion to make policies) *and* executive power (when they implement these policies). Administrators make value-based, ethical decisions, arguably with their discretion, compared with legislators, elected officials, who make fact-based decisions when they pass laws and statutes. Remember, these value-based decisions *should* be balancing between the values of the community and administrators' professionalism and expertise.[9] Morality comes into play when set against legal decisions.[10] What may be legal may not necessarily be moral. For example, the Supreme Court ruled that the *Kelo* taking was legal, but the morality of the decision, whether it was the *right* thing to do, continues to elicit controversy.

All of this relates to the idea of street-level bureaucrats, or the administrators that are actually involved in the implementation of the policy, the daily activities, have a better sense of the situation because of their proximity.[11] Alternatively, the case could be made that proximity may make it difficult for administrators' ability to appreciate fully the big picture, thus the need for balance between administrators and legislators in the process. Consider the idea of administrators as specialists (based on professional development, training, education, expertise, and experience) and legislators as generalists (jack-of-all-trades). Specialization may come at a cost, a trade-off, in terms of being inherently bounded in the ability to make decisions: depth at the expense of breadth, as well as time and resource constraints associated with government. These exert influence and pressure on administrators to *make decisions*, rather than to make necessarily the *best decision*.[12]

PROFESSIONALISM

Administrators' professionalism *should* be what helps them to exercise their discretion. At the foundation, professionalism should be normatively grounded, with a focus on how decisions *should* be made.[13] But this cannot be accomplished without a strong acknowledgment of the political context in which decisions are made. If the saying "all politics are local" holds true, which it most certainly does with eminent domain, then professionalism involves a balancing of: 1. the practitioners' professional development and training, expertise and competence, education, and professional experience that cultivate values and ethics with 2. the reflection of the community's values (the public interest, most broadly construed) with 3. the political environment. Especially with eminent domain, the community perspective should not be under-valued.[14]

Administrators' role in the decision-making process may be thought of as two-fold: a constitutive role and an instrumental role. The constitutive role is of making policy is derived from expertise and competency, which is inherently in tension with the instrumental role of implementing policies.[15] Tension persists because of the separation of powers between making policy and implementing policy. Checks and balances, however, help to alleviate this tension by acknowledging that these roles often overlap, especially at the local level of government.[16] Administrators should be proactive, seeking to build trust with the community, because of their expertise and competence.[17] Proactivity, however, should be balanced by prudent administrative behavior.[18]

Administrators are active participants in the development of policy, as well as the implementation process. They participate in policy-making when they use their discretion to make decisions by interpreting vague policies. Much of this is attributed to practitioners' presumed expertise and competence, or their professionalism. This is useful to understanding the relationships of professionalism and discretionary activities.

IMPLEMENTATION OF A LEGAL CASE

Implementing a legal case is no simple task. Since *Kelo*, forty-three states enacted or revised their eminent domain statutes. The implementation of a legal case, therefore, involves administrators' discretion and professionalism in determining how to put *Kelo* into practice. In other words, practitioners are having to take something as high-level as a Supreme Court decision, which legislators have then vaguely applied to their entire state in a revised statute, and determine what that means for their local government. Talk about discretion in action!

To implement a legal case, administrators use discretion to interpret the policies by balancing legal compliance with ethical judgment.[19] Building trust necessitates the importance of good-faith implementation efforts.[20] Despite the boundedness of practitioners' decision-making abilities, they should attempt to address all of the relevant factors, which may involve further professional development and training.[21]

Implementing constitutional principles includes an emphasis on practitioners' active use of discretion to assess, clarify, and problem-solve.[22] Accountable deliberation that should involve a balancing of regulatory goals and norms of constitutional dimensions is essential to the process.[23] What all of this means is that administrators rely on their discretion and professionalism to balance the legal issues of compliance with the ethical components involved in making complex decisions. For example, with eminent domain, implementing *Kelo* means that administrators should work to balance the vague, state-wide laws are on eminent domain with the particular characteristics of their communities.

PUBLIC SERVICE MOTIVATION

Practitioners' motivations for public service cannot be ignored as a factor contributing to their exercise of administrative discretion: public service motivation has been called the "public service ethic."[24] Over the years, research has evolved with regard to the development of ways to measure administrators' motives for public service. These include an emphasis on the intrinsic motivations, including: concern for the welfare of the community, consider public service a civic duty, desire to serve the public interest, financial security, opportunity to champion public issues, and participation in the process of program or policy formulation.[25]

COMPLEMENTARITY OF POLITICS AND ADMINISTRATION

Politics and administration, or the political pressures exerted on administrators when they use their discretion to implement policies, is often debated regarding whether they are, or should be, truly separate pieces of the governance process.[26] Such a divide might make sense in theory (e.g., that the legislative branch makes the laws that the executive branch them implements), it is impractical in practice. The relationship between politics and administration, or the complementarity of the two, holds that the relationship between elected officials and administrators is characterized by "interdependency, extensive interaction, distinct but overlapping roles, and political supremacy and administrative subordination."[27] At the local level of government, the relationship between elected officials and administrators "coexist with reciprocity of influence in both policy-making and administration."[28]

Research shows that, although the roles and actions of elected officials and administrators are not entirely blended, they substantially extend beyond what a strict separation between politics and administration.[29] During the policy-making process, elected officials and administrators share the responsibility. This is most clearly shown in what is called the zone of complementarity. Here, administrators enjoy a high degree of independence, while elected officials maintain a fairly high degree of control. The reciprocal nature of this relationship exists because elected officials "respect administrative competence and commitment" and because "administrators are committed to accountability and responsiveness."[30] Further, the emphasis on administrators and elected officials working together in the development and implementation of policies is significant. To understand relationships between practitioners' professionalism and discretion necessitates an understanding of the political context in which these decisions must be made.

PUBLIC GOOD V. PUBLIC INTEREST

When exercising discretion to implement policies, administrators' balancing act engages a complex equation of their professionalism (and values) with the values of the community (and the political context in which they are operating). Public administrators often use some notion of the public interest to help them figure out whether a decision they make will be a good one for the community they serve. Perhaps the only thing *more* vague that post-*Kelo* eminent domain policies is the public interest. Oh, wait, these policies often *refer* the public interest as being a qualifier for takings. Sometimes, these policies use another similarly vague phrase, the public good.

Readers should not expect to find a hard-and-fast definition of either public interest or public good in this book. Such definitions do not exist. Nor should they. The very notion of the public interest, or the public good, is that *it depends*. The meaning and practical value of the public interest/public good depends on the specific context in which the decision is being made, on the political landscape of the community, on what is in the interest/for the good of the community that the public administrator is serving.

That being said, there are some useful distinctions between public interest and public good, as well as characteristics of each, that may be helpful to practitioners. This discussion is meant to foster discussion and critical analysis about how administrators use their discretion to implement policies. Eminent domain policies may prove especially challenging because state statutes often use public interest and public good (and public purpose and public use) in ways without clear intention or substantial guidance.[31]

Consider public good and public interest as they relate to one another, as comparison is an easy way to point out distinctions. Public good is often thought of as being encompassed in a much broader public interest.[32] In other words, the public good may be "derivative from" the public interest, not "constitutive of" it.[33] Related to this is the idea that public interest is more subjectively-based, compared with the objective nature of the public good.[34]

There is also a difference regarding the more objective benefits and subjective, or desired, policy outcomes associated with the public interest, whereas the public good is more narrowly focused, at the expense of broadly considering those whom the policy is bound to affect. What this means is that administrators possess a heightened awareness of the "affectively desired outcomes" of a policy decision when the public interest is invoked.[35] The public good, however, limits awareness to tangible, intended outcomes.

Consider public interest and public good from a constitutional perspective, appropriate, given that the power of eminent domain is granted to the government in the Constitution.[36] This approach emphasizes the evolution of public good to public interest. The framers of our Constitution favored public or common good and general welfare, rather than public interest, attributed to the objectiveness of the public good.[37] Public good evolved into public interest as society became concerned with material benefits and an individualistic notion of public good, attributed to increased demands for private property protections.[38]

GOVERNANCE PROCESS

Governance is "the administration of public affairs in a political context."[39] It is the broad environment in which public administrators exercise their discretion, being mindful of professionalism and the political context of their community. According to a former United States president (who was an academic researcher first!): "Administration is the most obvious part of government; it is government in action."[40] This is especially true at the local level of government. Community members interact far more with local government officials and administrators than they do with their state or federal government. In local government, those who govern are often neighbors and colleagues, they are *real people* that community members interact with on a frequent basis.

When these administrators are faced with tough decisions involving their use of discretion, they have to try first to figure out what their role in the process will be. Before practitioners can use their discretion, they have to admit to themselves that they even have it in the first place. This is the antithesis to "passing the buck." Practitioners should consider three things: the perspective of the agency or local government department in which they are employed, the constitutional constraints and rule of law, and that public service is a calling. Some formulation of the public interest or the public good that is gives due attention to community values should also be emphasized.[41]

Other ideas about the governance process focus on achieving controls, direction, and coordination among people and departments. Part of this comes from acknowledging administrative discretion in addition to the formal authority, an acknowledgement that should be made by the practitioners themselves, as well as other administrators in the government.[42] But this exercise of discretion in the bureaucracy should be tempered with the presence of democratic elements.[43] In the case of eminent domain, for example, administrative discretion on the implementation of takings policies (what the government thinks is a good decision for the community) with the inclusion of public participation (in the form of public hearings to express their desires). When discretion is corrupted or abused, by either the administrator, the local government, or another organization higher up on the food chain, the balance may be shifted at the expense of local autonomy and control (as was the case in *Kelo*).

Public administrators may be viewed as "groping along" through the governance process, but that is the very nature of the system that was designed to protect individual rights through a deliberative, transparent process.[44] This process *should* be "post-bureaucratic," or one that legitimizes authority in both public administration and society.[45] The means of how to balance bureaucracy with democracy may remain blurry for practitioners, but the ends should be practitioners being responsible to professional standards and the public interest.[46] Government is a complex environment for administrators to navigate, given the "excess of procedural rules."[47]

These procedural rules, however, may be thought of more broadly as the rule of law. Rule of law is a fundamental distinguishing attribute of public administration.[48] Practitioners should share their role in governance *with* community members; practitioners' role should be normatively grounded in the rule of law.[49] What this amounts to is administrators balancing considerations of the way decisions *should* be made with the legal boundaries.

Rather than viewing the rule of law as burdensome constraints, consider more positive, thought-provoking constructions. Regime values of freedom, property, and equality help guide practitioners in understanding and interpreting the rule of law.[50] Societal values that have endured over time may be a good starting point as an indicator.[51] Or think about the "principle dimensions" of laws to help assess policies with an emphasis on improving citizens' lives.[52]

And then there is the red-tape argument. We have all heard it, that the government is inflexible and unresponsive. But government can also be innovative and grounded in a public-values approach.[53] Practitioners should be responsive to the public interest, while at the same time being responsible to make the tough decisions. Government is supposed to be representative of the public for just these reasons.[54] These are called the three Rs: responsiveness, responsibility, and representativeness. Often times with eminent domain, as evidenced by the public controversy, these take a back seat to the three Es: economy, efficiency, and effectiveness.[55] The Rs and the Es should work *together* as a focus for practitioners, as they have a mutually-reinforcing relationship that can strengthen the others.

The frequent triumph of the three Es over the three Rs has a much broader negative impact: the publicness of public service is being diminished by the focus on making government run more like a business. Neglecting of a fourth E, equity, sharpens the decline of public-values.[56] This then leads to practitioners assuming a more passive role in the governance process, resulting in decreased public accountability and transparency.

In the *Kelo* takings, this proved to be harmful because many of the key players were from the private sector. The word "corporation" was even in the name of the public-private partnership organization that did the actual taking of private property. This is actually a fairly common practice, that local governments will grant authority to a redevelopment agent to help them with using eminent domain. Organizations like this are so prevalent that they are called quasi-governmental organizations.[57] These types of arrangements usually occur because of the relatively small size and funding resources available to local governments; it becomes more cost-effective to contract out with private firms (which, in turn, saves taxpayers' money). It becomes problematic, however, when transparency dissolves and the local government gets swallowed up by the larger entity. Moreover, to whom are these organizations accountable? Lack of accountability is troubling because of the rule of law as being the fundamental distinction between public and private organizations.[58]

Now that all that is finished (exciting, right?), the focus of the book shifts toward the practice of eminent domain. Exploring the evolution of takings through Supreme Court rulings facilitates a balanced discussion of how eminent domain has manifested in practice over time. The low standards of the high Court begin to emerge.

NOTES

1. From Denhardt. Theories of Public Organization, 6E. © 2011 Wadsworth, a part of Cengage Learning, Inc. Reproduced by permission. www.cengage.com/permissions

2. Many thanks are owed to the students in my Public Policy Analysis class, taught during the spring 2011 semester at Shippensburg University: Mark Burke, Patrick Burnham, Tim Carr, Jenee Corsey, Eric Evans, Kyle Fagan, Chris Greene, Jasmine Henderson, Ryan Limes, Evan Nilsen, Travis Smith, Meagan Thorpe, and Rachael Unger, as well as to a good friend from graduate school, Mike Potter, now at Ap-

palachian State University, for fleshing out the idea of praxis and the amoeba that is public administration.

3. Denhardt (2011, p. 214).
4. See Figure 6.1: A Typology of Administrators' Discretion in chapter 6 for the application of these theories to the practice of eminent domain. The concepts covered in this chapter converge when administrators make decisions about whether and how to implement eminent domain and the process for doing so. Excercising the takings power involves a balancing act. This tension exists between being responsible about using eminent domain and its subsequent implications, which manifests as advancing the community through takings, and being responsive to the community, manifesting as public support or political fallout.
5. Rohr (1989).
6. Rohr (1989, pp. 36-37).
7. Dworkin (1967).
8. Behn (1998).
9. Simon (1997).
10. Foster (1981).
11. Lipsky (1980).
12. Simon (1997).
13. Green, Wamsley, & Keller (1993).
14. Chandler (1983).
15. Cook (1998).
16. Goodnow (2003); Wilson (1887).
17. Foster (1981).
18. Hart (1984).
19. Garofalo (2008).
20. Eubanks (2004).
21. Hunter (2004); Mawdsley (2000).
22. Gooden (2004).
23. Bamberger (2008).
24. Perry & Wise (1990, p. 370).
25. Perry (1996, 1997); Perry & Wise (1990).
26. Goodnow (2003); Wilson (1887).
27. Svara (1999a, p. 678).
28. Svara (1999a, p. 678).
29. Svara (1985, 1999a, 1999b, 2001).
30. Svara (2001, p. 179).
31. See Olejarski (2011b) for an in-depth analysis of post-*Kelo* state legislation.
32. Douglass (1980).
33. Morgan (2001, p. 152).
34. Goodsell (1990).
35. Goodsell (1990, p. 101).
36. Spicer & Terry (1993).
37. Morgan (2001, p. 152).

38. Douglass (1980).
39. Wamsley et al. (1990, p. 36).
40. Wilson (1887, p. 198).
41. Wamsley et al. (1990).
42. Lynn, Heinrich, & Hill (2000).
43. Meier (1997).
44. Behn (1995, p. 212)
45. Waldo (1952, p. 103).
46. Gaus (1936).
47. Behn (1995, p. 315).
48. Lynn (1998).
49. Wamsley et al. (1990, p. 36).
50. Rohr (1989).
51. Green (1992).
52. Long (1988, p. 341).
53. Goodsell (2004).
54. Krislov (1974).
55. Wamsley (1996).
56. Haque (2001).
57. Moe (2001).
58. Moe (2001).

Part II

EMINENT DOMAIN USES AND ABUSES

Part II explores the evolution of eminent domain via judicial interpretations that influence the practical application of takings. Legal precedents and established doctrines contributing to the present controversies surrounding eminent domain are presented in a clear way that explains the central issues to takings policies. Conceptual questions are also addressed.

Chapter Three

The Low Standards of the High Court

We emphasize that nothing in our opinion precludes any state from placing further restrictions on its exercise of the takings power.

—United States Supreme Court, *Kelo v. New London*

For students, practitioners, and scholars of public administration, rule of law is the fundamental distinguishing characteristic of the field. More specifically, the work of public administrators should be normatively grounded in the United States Constitution. Rule of law has evolved in our governance system to incorporate democratic ideals, like public participation, in the process.

This chapter explores the evolution of the legal side of eminent domain via the United States Supreme Court's landmark takings cases. Four cases will be examined with the goal of facilitating the emergence of themes and legal precedents. Consider this as a timeline dating back to the late 1800s, during which time the Court first discussed the public use controversy, to more recent decisions in the mid-1900s, on which the Court relied heavily in *Kelo*. This helps to understand how eminent domain has become one of public administration's most controversial issues.

"PUBLIC USE" DOES NOT MEAN USE BY THE PUBLIC

As early as 1896, the Court ruled that the public use requirement of the Takings Clause does not mean use by the public. In *Fallbrook Irrigation District v. Bradley*, the central issue was a California statute regarding the irrigation of arid land, in total about 600 million acres in the northwestern United

States, stretching from Colorado to the Pacific Ocean.[1] Artificial irrigation had been used on only about one million acres of land throughout the state.

This statute essentially provided for the creation of irrigation districts that would be managed by private corporations responsible for levying an assessment, or tax, on property owners in these arid conditions. The assessment, amounting to $6,000 in all, was to be used to irrigate artificially the land in the district. One property owner refused to pay this tax of $51.31.[2] California's law allowed the private corporation to enforce collection of the easement by selling the land, which it did.

Two important themes emerge from the Court's decision in *Fallbrook*: legislative deference and the earliest sighting of the public use as public purpose doctrine. The practice of legislative deference involves the Court relying on the policy decisions of state legislatures in the cases it hears. Here is an example from *Fallbrook*:

> The people of California and the members of her legislature must in the nature of things be more familiar with the facts and circumstances which surround the subject and with the necessities and the occasion for the irrigation of the lands than can anyone who is a stranger to her soil.[3]

What this means is that the Court strongly considers the decisions of the state legislature during the process of making its ruling in a case. The Court's basis for this deference is that the legislative body of a state is in a better position to evaluate the content and context of a particular situation because they are more knowledgeable and more familiar. Justice Peckham, in writing the opinion of the Court, continues to assert that legislatures' "knowledge and familiarity must have their due weight. . . ."[4]

Contributing even more to the present controversies surrounding eminent domain is the emergence of the public use as public purpose doctrine. The Takings Clause includes the public use requirement: "Nor shall private property be taken for public use, without just compensation." With the Court's decision in *Fallbrook,* we begin to see the earliest signs of a broader interpretation of public use as public purpose. The public use issue in the case centers around the water used for artificial irrigation of land in the district. Because the water would not be used domestically and would be limited to the irrigation and subsequent crop cultivation of otherwise useless land, the Court ruled that it constituted a public use.

On one hand, we have the public use requirement of the Takings Clause. On the other, however, is the Court's operationalization in practice. In *Fallbrook,* the Court maintains, "It is not essential that the entire community or even any considerable portion thereof should directly enjoy or participate in an improvement in order to constitute a public use."[5] This is one of the most oft-cited judicial references in support of expanding interpretations of public use to public purpose.

Missing from these claims, however, is due attention to the nuanced, limiting nature of the Court's quote. Certainly, at face value, it appears as though the Court is asserting that public use does not mean use by the public. More important is the immediately following sentence, "The water is not used for general, domestic, or drinking purposes, and it is plain from the scheme of the act that the water is intended for the use of those who will have occasion to use it on their lands."[6]

The public use requirement of the Takings Clause, as interpreted by the Court in *Fallbrook*, does not require every member of the public to have direct use of the land being taken. It does engage, however, the requirement regarding every relevant member of the public. In other words, the Court's operationalization of public use here requires that the public with any cause or motivation to use the land should have access to it. Misappropriations of the Court's interpretation of the meaning of public use have evolved into a far broader public purpose in contemporary decisions. In the 2005 *Kelo* decision, the Court relied on its *Fallbrook* ruling in interpreting public use as public purpose.

BLIGHT REMOVAL FOR "VARIED PURPOSES"

Fast-forward to Washington, DC, in 1954 with the Court's unanimous (9-0) decision in *Berman v. Parker*.[7] At issue was the District of Columbia Redevelopment Act of 1945, which empowered DC to use eminent domain to remove blight. As with *Fallbrook*, the Court continued its practice of legislative deference. Also particularly significant for public administration is that the issue of public use v. public purpose barely made an appearance, beyond citing the act in question's determination that blight removal constitutes a public use. Throughout the *Berman* decision, it was just public purpose, with little discussion questioning the validity. Most notably in *Berman*, however, is the Court's equating the power of eminent domain with the police power to maintain health, safety, and morality.

The first blight removal project of the act dealt with a predominantly residential neighborhood of about 5,000 residents, of which 97.5 percent were black. In this particular area of Washington, DC, the figures supporting blight claims make a strong case with regard to the properties: 64.3 percent were beyond repair, 18.4 percent needed major repairs, and 17.3 percent were deemed satisfactory; 57.8 percent had outside toilets, 60.3 percent had no baths, 29.3 percent lacked electricity, 82.2 percent had no laundry tubs, and

83.3 percent lacked central heating.[8] DC determined that these conditions amounted to public health concerns that needed to be remediated.[9]

Although the public use as public purpose issue assumed a central role in *Fallbrook*, the Court hardly discussed the question in *Berman*, noting that the uses for redeveloped land were for "varied purposes," only specifying that one-third be for low-rent housing.[10] One property owner in the targeted land disputed the use of eminent domain, asserting that his land was commercial, a department store, and that it was not blighted. He continued to argue that his property would be taken and turned over to a private firm, allowed by the DC act, and put to private use.

In *Berman*, the Court continued its practice of legislative deference, taking a much stronger stance on the question of the legislative v. judicial oversight:

> Subject to specific constitutional limitations, when the legislature has spoken, the public interest has been declared in terms of well-nigh conclusive. In such cases the legislature, not the judiciary, is the main guardian of the public needs to be served by social legislation. . . .[11]

Here, the Court created an inextricable link between legislative deference and police power. The so-called police power refers to localities' responsibility to regulate "public safety, public health, morality, peace and quiet, [and] law and order."[12] Because Washington, DC, determined that the blighted conditions amounted to a public health concern, the Court ruled that eminent domain was a justifiable action through which to assert its police power:

> This principle [of the police power] admits of no exception merely because the power of eminent domain is involved. The role of the judiciary in determining whether the power [of eminent domain] is being exercised for a public purpose is an extremely narrow one.[13]

Important to understand in this relationship between the governmental police power and the execution of that power via eminent domain are two issues. First, the Court maintains that the judiciary should take a back-seat to the legislature in determining how to serve best its constituency. Second, the Court aptly notes that their role in the process is narrow and surfaces when constitutional limitations appear.

Again, the Takings Clause of the Constitution includes the public use requirement for takings. That the Court acknowledges their active role in the presence of constitutional limitations, combined with the constitutional limitation that eminent domain be employed for public use, shows that the public use as public purpose is little more than an afterthought in its *Berman* decision. Candidly, the Court emphasizes, "For the power of eminent domain is merely the means to the end."[14] This line of reasoning comes back to haunt the Court in its next eminent domain case, thirty years later.

What the Court essentially does in *Berman* is to assert itself into the process of judicial review in considerably limiting terms, otherwise deferring to the legislature. The *Fallbrook* decision that the legislature is closest to the situation, and, in turn, is most likely to be knowledgeable about the content and context of the use of eminent domain is now expanded even further. Now, after *Berman*, the Court largely side-steps the issue on the basis of the police power argument, noting, "We do not sit to determine whether a particular housing project is or is not desirable."[15]

The Court describes the rationale for equating the power of eminent domain with the police power as being broad in scope. This is a bit contradictory because if the police power should be broadly construed, how might that be reconciled with the inherently limiting character of the Takings Clause and the public use requirement? It is one thing to argue that the governmental police power necessitates great latitude in securing protections for citizens, but the power itself should be separated from the manner used to execute it, namely eminent domain.

The Court's discussion of the broad nature of the police power is interesting, for its description appears to be all-encompassing. Beginning with the more generally accepted notions of police power, such as the relationship between blighted housing conditions and crime and sanitation, the police power somehow extends to beautification efforts: "If those who govern the District of Columbia decide that the Nation's Capital should be beautiful as well as sanitary, there is nothing in the Fifth Amendment that stands in the way."[16]

A PRIVATE TRANSACTION MAY BE "RAISED TO A PUBLIC AFFAIR"

Thirty years later, the Court made its next landmark ruling in *Hawaii Housing Authority v. Midkiff* in 1984.[17] Like *Berman*, this decision was unanimous (8-0). In *Midkiff*, the Hawaiian legislature enacted the Land Reform Act of 1967, the details of which are more intricate than the DC redevelopment act in question with *Berman*. The Court relied heavily on the legal precedents it set from thirty years prior: broadly interpreting some degree of private benefit into the public-use equation and the severe practice of legislative deference. Quite important to note is that Justice O'Connor delivered the opinion of the Court in *Midkiff*, yet she wrote the dissenting opinion in the 2005 *Kelo* case. This is quite a shift from adamantly supporting eminent domain for economic development in this case and rallying against it in *Kelo*. I hope that you are wondering why. The short answer: *context*. Context is the key to making decisions about eminent domain because the solution depends on the landscape of the community in question.

Property ownership throughout the state of Hawaii was extremely concentrated to the point that the legislature feared market failure. Resulting from the lacking diversity of land ownership were inflated pricing, a skewing of the market, and monopoly conditions. According to data provided by the legislature, the figures throughout the state are staggering: the state and federal government owned 49 percent of land, and another 47 percent was owned by only seventy-two private individuals; eighteen land holders owned over 40 percent of that 47 percent. On the most urbanized island, twenty-two property owners held almost 73 percent of the titles.[18]

In order to diversify property ownership, the Hawaiian legislature enacted a land reform act. This statute allowed renters to have the property condemned by the state housing authority; after condemnation, renters would be able to purchase the property. Such was a compromise with the original property owners to minimize federal taxes associated with voluntary sales. Once the housing authority acquired the property, either by initiating eminent domain proceedings or through negotiation with the original property owner, the property would be sold to the renter. The housing authority was authorized to lend the renters up to 90 percent of the purchase price of the property, though at the time the case reached the Court, this practice had not actually been used at all because renters provided full funding. Further, the housing authority was not permitted to profit from the sale.

Here, the Court explicitly relied on its precedent ruling in *Berman* thirty years prior, stating: "The starting point for our analysis of the act's constitutionality is the Court's decision in *Berman v. Parker*."[19] In *Midkiff*, the Court addressed the police power argument in the form of reiterating lengthy quotations from *Berman*. It concluded, "The 'public use' requirement is thus coterminous with the scope of a sovereign's police powers."[20] This means that eminent domain falls under the category of an inherently governmental power, or one that the government can exercise as a police power (health, safety, morality, according to the Court).

Regarding the issue of private benefit into the public use requirement, the Court was quick to relate this to its historical practice of legislative deference in takings cases. In addition to again asserting its narrow role of judicial review, the Court introduces the idea that eminent domain must be "rationally related" to "a conceivable public purpose."[21] Although no further explanation is given as to what constitutes "rationality" or "conceivability," this is a sufficient standard for the Court. It should come as little surprise when the Court then concludes, "On this basis, we have no trouble concluding that the Hawaii Act is constitutional."[22] Also important here is the notion that eminent domain is constitutional even when private property is taken and then transferred to a private benefit: "What in its immediate aspect is only a private transaction may be raised by its class or character to a public affair."[23]

The *Midkiff* decision gets especially interesting as the Court begins to explain its rationale behind its severe practice of legislative deference in takings cases. One of the central issues in the Court's takings decisions has been its deference to legislative actions. In *Midkiff*, the Court aptly explains:

> Deference is required because, in our system of government, legislatures are better able to assess what public purposes should be advanced by an exercise of the takings power. . . . Thus, if a legislature, state or federal, determines that there are substantial reasons for an exercise of the takings power, courts must defer to its determination that the taking will serve a public purpose.[24]

The Court, therefore, makes it very clear that their role, self-described as narrow, in reviewing eminent domain cases is limited to the purpose of the taking, not the ways in which the taking is initiated or implemented, "It is only the takings purpose, and not its mechanics, that must pass scrutiny under the Public Use Clause."[25]

THE SUPREME COURT INVITES STATES TO "PLACE FURTHER RESTRICTIONS ON ITS EXERCISE OF THE TAKINGS POWER"

Unlike the unanimous decisions in *Berman* and *Midkiff*, the Court was divided 5-4 in its 2005 *Kelo v. New London* decision.[26] This four-opinion decision warrants a particularly in-depth discussion because it is based largely on the Court's precedents set forth in *Berman* and *Midkiff*, and it provides the most recent guidance on takings for public administrators. Justice Stevens delivered the *opinion* of the Court and was joined by Justices Kennedy, Souter, Ginsburg, and Breyer, with Kennedy filing a *concurring* opinion. Justice O'Connor filed a *dissenting* opinion, and Chief Justice Rehnquist and Justices Scalia and Thomas joined; Thomas also filed a *dissenting* opinion.

The petitioners in *Kelo* were not necessarily asking the Court to decide on an entirely new issue, but instead, to reexamine the eminent domain doctrines established in *Berman* and *Midkiff*. Most notably, the petitioners sought to have the Court evaluate the constitutionality of takings for economic development. Further, the Court addressed the broad v. narrow interpretation of public use in the Takings Clause, as well as whether the city's redevelopment plan served the public purpose. At issue again was the Court's historical practice of legislative deference.

The state of Connecticut designated the city of New London a "distressed municipality" in 1990.[27] In 1996, the federal government closed the Naval

Undersea Warfare Center that employed over 1,500 people.[28] By 1998, the city's unemployment rate had reached lows not seen since the 1920s. Economic redevelopment efforts began to focus on the city of New London and its Fort Trumbull neighborhood, in particular. The state approved bond funding of over $5 million to support the New London Development Corporation (NLDC)'s redevelopment planning efforts, as well as a $10 million bond to build a park in the area.

Pharmaceutical company Pfizer was the key to the city's economic redevelopment efforts, as it announced plans to build a $300 million research and development facility in the Fort Trumbull neighborhood. The idea was that bringing Pfizer to the community would increase jobs and tax revenue. The NLDC received state approval and began targeting ninety acres in the community for redevelopment. This ninety-acre plot included 115 private properties and thirty-two acres of land left vacant with the closing of the naval base. The area was divided into seven parcels: a conference hotel, restaurants, and shopping; eighty new residences and a Coast Guard museum; 90,000 square feet of research and development office space for Pfizer; parking and retail services to support the marina; and office and retail space and parking. It is very important to note that the purposes of the NLDC's redevelopment plan were described by the Court in the order listed here, with Pfizer's economic benefits first.

Economic considerations are at the heart of the case because the city, and in turn the Court, are once again granting a great degree of deference to state and local legislative actions and their interpretations of public use. The city and NLDC interpreted public use in the broadest sense of the term by listing the benefits gained by building the Pfizer facility ahead of the direct public use of the recreational facilities. That the Court accepted the redevelopment plan's purpose without further examination is not surprising, giving its historical practice of deference. Once again, the Court's narrow role of judicial review in takings cases therefore extends to ensuring that the procedural aspects of the taking are constitutional and defers to the legislature on issues regarding purpose.

Relying on the precedents established in *Berman* and *Midkiff*, the Court's decision continued its historical practice of legislative deference and broadly interpreting public use as public purpose. Justice Stevens's opinion for the Court stated: "Without exception, our cases have defined that concept [public use] broadly, reflecting our longstanding policy of deference to legislative judgments in this field."[29] Here, while acknowledging that the NLDC's redevelopment plan did not allow the public direct access to the land taken, Justice Stevens argued that there were costs associated with determining public v. private access based on changing community needs.

Though the line between public and private takings may be blurred, as long as the public benefits from the taking, via economic development in

Kelo, the taking is constitutional. The Court continued to assert that economic development is a traditional function of government and argued on behalf of states' rights to advance it through eminent domain. In one of the most oft-cited quotes from the *Kelo* decision, the Court hands decisions regarding the use of eminent domain for economic development right back to the states: "We emphasize that nothing in our opinion precludes any state from placing further restrictions on its exercise of the takings power."[30] In response to the Court's invitation, forty-three states have responded, enacting new or revised eminent domain legislation.[31]

Regarding the central question in *Kelo* of whether economic development met the public use requirement in the Constitution, the Court continued its practice of deferring to the state legislature, as well as precedent. Important here were two main policies: the Court's ruling in *Berman* and a Connecticut statute. In *Berman*, the Court decided that economic development is a constitutionally justifiable use for eminent domain. Moreover, the Court in *Kelo* relied on a state municipal redevelopment statute that allowed for the taking of developed land for economic development, holding that it does satisfy the public use requirement, and that such decisions should be determined by the state legislature. Justice Stevens's opinion for the Court stated:

> Those who govern the City were not confronted with the need to remove blight in the Fort Trumbull area, but their determination that the area was sufficiently distressed to justify a program of economic rejuvenation is entitled to our deference.[32]

Like in *Midkiff*, the Court asserted its role in evaluating takings cases to be a narrow one. Here, the issue once again centered on the broader issues associated with the purpose of the taking, rather than the mechanics; the *Kelo* decision cited this quotation directly from *Midkiff* to support their assertion. In the end, the Court decided: "Because that plan unquestionably serves a public purpose, the takings challenged here satisfy the public use requirement of the Fifth Amendment [of the Constitution]."[33]

Justice Kennedy's concurring opinion clarified the degree to which the public and private parties involved in the taking should benefit when he reiterated the incidental benefit principle. Kennedy explicitly stated that takings where the public benefit is only incidental are "forbidden" by the public use requirement of the Takings Clause.[34] He continued, maintaining that when accusations are made that takings were implemented in strong favor of the private parties involved, the Court has a responsibility to examine the case closely. This closer examination, however, should be conducted under the presumption that the taking was for public use and that the government's actions were reasonable.

Here, in *Kelo*, the petitioners' argument was two-fold: Their property was not blighted, and the proposed development on their property was not for the public use, in the narrow interpretation of the term excluding economic development. The Court responded that it was not feasible to examine economic development takings on an individual basis. Although not all of the land in the taking was blighted, that the community was declared distressed and the redevelopment plan sought to revitalize the community was sufficient. Justice Stevens stated, "Just as we decline to second-guess the City's considered judgments about the efficacy of its development plan, we also decline to second-guess the City's determinations as to what land it needs to acquire to effectuate the project."[35]

Because the Court found the city's redevelopment plan to be comprehensive and the petitioners' legal rights had been protected, heightening judicial review would cause an unnecessary and unfeasible burden on the implementation of the redevelopment efforts. Essentially, the petitioners were asking the Court to require a direct, visible public benefit for each individual property that was taken. Not only did the Court view the petitioners' new review as imposing unreasonable time constraints on the state, but it also disqualified the argument on the basis of the existing statute that protected the state's use of eminent domain, therefore invalidating additional, individual assurances.

Remember that Justice O'Connor delivered the dissenting opinion for the Court, and she was joined by Chief Justice Rehnquist and Justices Scalia and Thomas. O'Connor's dissent embraced the idea that after the *Kelo* decision, private property would be unsafe from takings for private development, as it could be condemned in a taking simply because the state identified an alternative use that would be more beneficial to the public or a range of parties. In her *Kelo* dissent, Justice O'Connor equated the decision to "effectively delet[ing] the words 'for public use' from the Takings Clause of the Fifth Amendment."[36]

Justice O'Connor argued that because nearly all private property could potentially generate some form of public benefit, the Court's decision to extend its practice of legislative deference without an additional heightened judicial review eliminated any constraints on governmental takings. She distinguished between the perceived and actual reasons for the petitioners' suit against the city in order to clarify the basis for her opinion. It was not that the petitioners were opposed to the redevelopment efforts or holding out for higher compensation; they were opposed to the lack of a direct public benefit, or the public use required in the Constitution. A key problem addressed in the dissenters' argument was the idea that, after *Kelo*, private property could be taken merely because someone else, another private owner, could be more productive or beneficial with it in the eyes of the government. Justice O'Connor argued in her dissent:

> The Court rightfully admits, however, that the judiciary cannot get bogged down in predictive judgments about whether the public will actually be better off after a property transfer. In any event, this constraint has no realistic import. For who among us can say she already makes the most productive or attractive possible use of her property? The specter of condemnation hangs over all property. Nothing is to prevent the state from replacing any Motel 6 with a Ritz Carlton, any home with a shopping mall, or any farm with a factory.[37]

Justice O'Connor favored establishing some mechanism to evaluate individually private property in economic development takings. Citing *Berman*, she argued that because all of the properties were blighted, the public benefit was clear. In *Kelo*, however, this was not the case; she was cautious of the government's expanded power to condemn unblighted private property purely for economic development.

The dissenting opinions give much more attention to the specific details of the city's redevelopment plan than did the majority opinion. Two of the seven parcels of land scheduled for redevelopment were occupied by the petitioners. In one parcel, the three existing homes were to be condemned, but the existing Italian Dramatic Club (a private men's club, housed ironically in a pink building) would remain; future plans for this parcel were vague and slated for office space as the market developed. Future plans for the other parcel where petitioners resided were more ambiguous, as it was listed "mysteriously, for park support."[38] The dissent cited oral arguments during which the city conceded that the area could potentially be used for parking, a use the dissent argued did not meet the public use requirement of the Takings Clause.

Recall that in the *Midkiff* opinion, Justice O'Connor stated that the state's power to invoke eminent domain was coterminous with that of its police power. In her *Kelo* dissent, she argued that the coterminousness of the two terms sometimes lacks constitutional muster that requires additional consideration. She explains that in *Midkiff*, the takings were both within the police power and for the public purpose and therefore did not put the coterminous language to the constitutional test. Moreover, in *Midkiff*, Justice O'Connor advocated for the judiciary to play a narrow role in reviewing takings cases, therefore adhering to the Court's practice of legislative deference.

In response to the Court's invitation that states enact stricter eminent domain legislation, Justice O'Connor sharply remarked:

> This is an abdication of our responsibility. States play many important functions in our system of dual sovereignty, but compensating for our refusal to enforce properly the Federal Constitution (and a provision meant to curtail state action, no less) is not among them.[39]

While acknowledging the role the states play in identifying limits on economic development takings, she encouraged the Court to fulfill its duty of judicial review and to uphold the Constitution.

Justice Thomas concurred with O'Connor's dissent and echoed her arguments that the Court's deference to the legislature resulted in an abdication of its judicial responsibility to protect individual Constitutional rights. He filed an additional dissent that recommended more extreme measures in curtailing the Court's broad interpretation of public use as public purpose to protect private property rights. Justice Thomas argued for a strict adherence to the public use requirement of the Takings Clause, and, in turn, a reexamination of the Court's historical rulings on public use cases.

In his dissenting opinion, Justice Thomas stated:

> It is far easier to analyze whether the government owns or the public has a legal right to use the taken property than to ask whether the taking has a "purely private purpose," unless the Court means to eliminate public use scrutiny of takings entirely. Obliterating a provision of the Constitution, of course, guarantees that it will not be misapplied. For all these reasons, I would revisit our Public Use Clause cases and consider returning to the original meaning of the Public Use Clause: that the government may take property only if it actually uses or gives the public a legal right to use the property.[40]

Justice Thomas viewed the public use and just compensation requirements of the Takings Clause to constrain strictly governmental uses of eminent domain, citing the remainder of the Constitution. The basis for Thomas's argument was: if the framers of the Constitution intended public use to be interpreted as public purpose, they would have explicitly stated that. He concluded that the Court's rulings in favor of a broader interpretation than the Constitution explicitly states should be *reconsidered.*

Now that legal precedents and established doctrines affecting the present controversies surrounding eminent domain have been analyzed, the next chapter shifts focus toward what happens *after the case*. Takings questions left unanswered, which I am broadly categorizing as constitutional and procedural issues, are briefly explored in the following chapter. What this highlights is the absence of a focus on the people actually involved with eminent domain, practitioners of public administration and community members, as well as the most controversial polemics.

NOTES

1. *Fallbrook Irrigation District v. Bradley,* 164 U.S. 112 (1896).

2. According to the "Purchasing power of money in the United States" calculator, found online at www.measuringworth.com, this 1896 $51.31 amounts to $1,350.00 in the year 2009.

3. *Fallbrook v. Bradley* (1896, p. 160).
4. *Fallbrook v. Bradley* (1896, p. 160).
5. *Fallbrook v. Bradley* (1896, pp. 161–162).
6. *Fallbrook v. Bradley* (1896, p. 162).
7. *Berman et al., Executors v. Parker et al.,* 348 U.S. 26 (1954).
8. *Berman v. Parker* (1954, p. 30).
9. Washington, DC's legislative activities are determined by the U.S. Congress.
10. *Berman v. Parker* (1954, pp. 30–31).
11. *Berman v. Parker* (1954, p. 32).
12. *Berman v. Parker* (1954, p. 32).
13. *Berman v. Parker* (1954, p. 32).
14. *Berman v. Parker* (1954, p. 32).
15. *Berman v. Parker* (1954, p. 32).
16. *Berman v. Parker* (1954, p. 33).
17. *Hawaii Housing Authority et al. v. Midkiff et al.,* 467 U.S. 229 (1984).
18. *Hawaii v. Midkiff* (1984).
19. *Hawaii v. Midkiff* (1984, p. 239).
20. *Hawaii v. Midkiff* (1984, p. 240).
21. *Hawaii v. Midkiff* (1984, p. 241).
22. *Hawaii v. Midkiff* (1984, p. 241).
23. *Hawaii v. Midkiff* (1984, p. 244).
24. *Hawaii v. Midkiff* (1984, p. 244).
25. *Hawaii v. Midkiff* (1984, p. 244).
26. *Kelo et al. v. City of New London et al.*, 545 U.S. 469 (2005).
27. *Kelo v. New London* (2005, p. 473).
28. The community members who participated in this study asserted that the figures cited in the case exaggerated the situation, particularly because not all of the naval base employees who lost their jobs with the closing were residents of the city.
29. *Kelo v. New London* (2005, p. 480).
30. *Kelo v. New London* (2005, p. 489).
31. See Olejarski (2011b) for detailed analysis of the post-*Kelo* state legislative response.
32. *Kelo v. New London* (2005, p. 483).
33. *Kelo v. New London* (2005, p. 484).
34. *Kelo v. New London* (2005, p. 490).
35. *Kelo v. New London* (2005, p. 488).
36. *Kelo v. New London* (2005, p. 494).
37. *Kelo v. New London* (2005, p. 503).
38. *Kelo v. New London* (2005, p. 495).
39. *Kelo v. New London* (2005, p. 504).
40. *Kelo v. New London* (2005, p. 521).

Chapter Four

A Narrative of Eminent Domain: Procedural or Constitutional?

After exploring the legal side of eminent domain, as put into practice by the Supreme Court in their takings rulings, this chapter briefly explores some of the most important issues brought to light from a different perspective. While much attention has been given to the rule of law regarding eminent domain, there are broader factors that practitioners, students, and scholars of public administration, as well as community members, should consider. In this chapter, relevant questions left unanswered on constitutional and procedural issues surrounding eminent domain are reviewed. Doing so facilitates a more practical understanding of eminent domain and provides much-needed context to understand what is fueling the takings debate. This grounds the debate as a public-service related issue, rather than a purely emotional issue.

What is missing from the existing takings research is an emphasis on the people, both public administrators and community members, actually involved in eminent domain. Because the goal of this book is to help educate practitioners and citizens (and students and scholars) on important issues about administrative discretion and eminent domain, this brief discussion begins to bridge gaps in the conversation. Seeing what others have written and researched on the subject provides a fuller picture of the complexity and nuances associated with eminent domain. This chapter also provides a host of resources for the interested reader.

OVERVIEW OF EMINENT DOMAIN RESEARCH

Research on eminent domain is dominated by law reviews, followed distantly by urban affairs and planning scholarship and research in the discipline of political science. Hardly anything has been written in the field of public administration. This research emphasizes constitutional issues of public use and just compensation, as well as a more procedural focus on transaction costs associated with takings and property valuation.

Also studied is the legislative environment, with a number of studies exploring the institutional or legislative shifts after *Kelo*, in addition to *Berman* and *Midkiff*. A good deal of research has been conducted on the historical context of eminent domain, dating back to seventeenth century conceptions of takings. Far less research has been done in recent history to evaluate the public's response to *Kelo*. There are some studies that attempt to provide a model or practical guide to implementing eminent domain.

CONSTITUTIONAL + PROCEDURAL = WHAT ABOUT THE PEOPLE ACTUALLY INVOLVED WITH EMINENT DOMAIN?

Research conducted on eminent domain may be broadly categorized into two streams: constitutional and procedural. The constitutional stream of research focuses mostly on issues of public use and just compensation. This body of research seeks to answer questions involving when and why eminent domain should be used. Alternatively, the procedural stream offers a more technical, mechanical approach, emphasizing the costs, tangible and intangible, associated with initiating and implementing eminent domain; procedural research asks questions surrounding how eminent domain should be used.

All of this study of constitutional and procedural issues has minimal practical value if the context is not provided. This is the value of case-study research, to provide a thick description of the nuances of a particular situation in the hopes of learning valuable practical lessons, as well as helping to build theories. People interested in administrative discretion and eminent domain should find no shortage of details in the following chapters.

CONSTITUTIONAL QUESTIONS OF PUBLIC USE AND JUST COMPENSATION

Recall Justice O'Connor's dissenting opinion in *Kelo* in which she asserted that the Court's decision essentially eliminated, or obliterated, in Justice Thomas's dissent, the public use requirement of the Fifth Amendment of the Constitution. This point was not lost on scholars, as it is resonated in a number of studies. Substantial judicial review, rather than the self-described narrow review of the Court in *Kelo*, can eliminate governmental limits on its power of eminent domain.[1] Even though the Court ruled in *Berman* that economic development is a constitutionally justifiable exercise of eminent domain, there is a distinction from urban revitalization, which comes closer to meeting the public-use requirement of the Constitution.[2] One argument asserts that takings for economic development should be banned if they are not for public use, while another is that eminent domain should be ruled unconstitutional if the purpose is private development.[3] Still, public-private partnerships provide an added value to broad conceptions of public purpose from saving tax dollars; some research favors economic development takings even in situations involving private gain for just this reason.[4] Regarding the public-use requirement of the Takings Clause, perhaps public benefit is more appropriate, based on the original intent of the Takings Clause.[5] This constitutional debate also extends to whether the takings requirements serve to protect marginalized citizens.[6] And, of course, the argument can be made that eminent domain for economic development, as well as broad interpretations of public use to include increased tax revenue, job growth, and community redevelopment, as was the case in *Kelo*.[7]

The Court's decision in *Kelo* was a collision of two of its landmark takings cases, *Berman* and *Midkiff*. *Berman* was the first time the Court ruled that economic development takings were constitutional; in *Midkiff*, private gain was permitted to overshadow the public use requirement. The public use as public purpose doctrine, coupled with the Court's narrow role of judicial review of the mechanics and purpose of takings, underscores the importance of identifying how public administrators understand eminent domain. Two central questions brought to light here include: the broad interpretation of public use as public purpose, as well as the narrow review of the mechanics and purpose of takings.

With the erosion of the public use requirement of the Takings Clause some researchers have argued that the just compensation requirement offers the only remaining protection for private property.[8] This is bolstered by arguments that the just compensation requirement serves as an incentive to limit governmental takings.[9] A *major* flaw in the just compensation requirement, however, is that it is based on the market-value of the property, which fails to consider the objective value to property owners.[10]

The Court has ruled that just compensation is equal to fair market value, which it defines as "what a willing buyer would pay in cash to a willing seller at the time of the taking."[11] This definition is troubling for a number of reasons: "Just compensation [as currently formulated] is not intended to cover every loss that a condemnee may suffer."[12] Interpretations of just compensation is broadening beyond fair market value to include relocation assistance, or a "percentage kicker" for homeowners or "loss of goodwill" for business owners.[13] In response to the problem of just compensation, alternative models have been proposed, including self-assessment, private-sector secret buying agents, over-appraisal findings, and pre-condemnation bargaining.[14]

Because just compensation is one of only two requirements in the Takings Clause, it is important to learn how this concept is understood. This is particularly relevant in light of scholars' focus on alternatives to the market-value approach and the role of the subjective value to property owners. Such may be helpful to strengthen the models, create benchmarks, and share information on potential strategies. The two key issues addressed by this body of research include: just compensation as a heightened standard in light of the erosion of the public use requirement, as well as exploring alternative compensation models and conceptions.

PROCEDURAL QUESTIONS OF TRANSACTION COSTS AND OVERSIGHT

Reviewing similar issues, research in the procedural stream emphasizes the transaction costs associated with initiating eminent domain proceedings, as well as questions surrounding takings oversight. A government's power to exercise eminent domain prevents holdouts from disrupting economic redevelopment efforts in such cases. While a holdout may be able to slow the condemnation process, "The legal availability of condemnation ensures that the sale will occur at something approaching market value."[15] Frequently, eminent domain proceedings are initiated specifically to circumvent holdouts.[16]

In other words, property owners who choose not to sell their property to the government for just compensation are able to slow, but not stop, the process. Once the government initiates eminent domain proceedings, the property will be taken. This process, however, results in significant transaction costs for the government, such as procedural due process litigation costs. While eminent domain can be useful for increasing property tax revenues and for minimizing litigation-based redevelopment delays, the associated transaction costs are then transferred to the public.[17] These additional costs incurred by the government may serve to limit takings.[18] Alternatively, property owners may be paid just compensation above market value because of the increases in efficiency and equity.[19]

The inefficiency of transaction costs resulting from eminent domain litigation is counter-productive to governments' goal of advancing the public good with takings. By passing along the additional costs, the public is affected by increased taxes and decreased governmental trust. The two significant issues highlighted by this stream of research include: inefficiency of transaction costs and balancing governmental goals.

The Court's practice of deference to state legislatures was significantly important in its *Kelo* decision. As explained by the Court, their self-described narrow role of judicial review regarding the purpose and mechanics of eminent domain is absent substantial evaluation extending beyond the broad purpose of the taking. A major issue in the procedural research studies whether the review of takings should come from the judicial or legislative branch of government. Essentially, this research focuses on the degree of regulation that is appropriate, compared with the governmental flexibility to advance the public good using eminent domain. Scholars make sound claims on both sides of the argument. On one hand, the argument explains, authority should rest with local governments to determine private-property protections. Such protection, he argues, should combine a cost-benefit balance of the taking.[20] On the other hand, however, there have been big-picture institutional shifts after *Kelo*, such as a tempering of governmental restrictions post-*Kelo*.[21] An oft-cited argument maintains that local governments have the flexibility to initiate eminent domain proceedings without being second-guessed by the judiciary.[22] Still, the property owner's perspective should be considered when making decisions regarding eminent domain.[23] Flexibility of local governments is important, but it should be kept in check with heightened governmental accountability.[24] Accountability may come in the form of the judicial branch requiring a means-ends scrutiny of local governments to limit their takings power without removing all flexibility.[25] Related to this idea is one suggesting procedural reforms, rather than those of the legislative nature.[26] A similar notion is that there should be strong legislative deference but also an increased standard of judicial review when there is only an indirect public benefit.[27] While stronger judicial review is emphasized by some, others call for the judiciary to administer a public-use test to limit the government's use of eminent domain.[28]

The Court's deference to state legislatures in *Kelo*, and the subsequent response of state legislatures to enact takings policies, becomes, by default, a deference to public administrators. This presents practitioners with a great opportunity to implement eminent domain policy in a way that is balanced and incorporates a tempering of traditional, constitutional perspectives with historical values.[29] Through their discretion, practitioners are charged with implementing vague and sometimes conflicting eminent domain legislation and subsequently with initiating eminent domain proceedings, optimistically in a manner inclusive of tangible benefits to the public, or the principle of tangibility.[30] The two important issues in this body of research include: deference to practitioners and the implementation of eminent domain regarding governmental flexibility and oversight.

This brief coverage of the questions surrounding eminent domain controversies paves the way for exploring praxis, or what all of this means to using discretion to implement eminent domain, in the next chapter. The following section of the book presents a balanced approach to understanding eminent domain from the perspective of community members and practitioners. Rather than attempting a polemic, the book attempts to educate and facilitate productive, transparent dialogue on takings. Both sides of the eminent domain debate have valid concerns, and the goal is to explore and begin to explain each side in a way that is practically useful. Public administrationists should find the empirical findings useful in developing a comprehensive, big-picture understanding of administrative discretion in the implementation of eminent domain.

NOTES

1. Bell & Parchomovsky (2007); Christensen (2005); Main (2005).
2. Han (2008).
3. Cohen (2006); Boudreaux (2005).
4. Salkin & Lucero (2005).
5. Melton (1996).
6. Boudreaux (2005); Goodin (2007); Mushkatel & Nakhleh (1978).
7. Farjad (2007).
8. Bell & Parchomovsky (2007).
9. Bell & Parchomovsky (2007); Esposto (1996); Fawcett (1986); Fee (2006); Gallagher (2005); Harrington (2002).
10. Durham (1985); Farjad (2007); Lehavi & Licht (2007); Myers (1997); Odabashian (2002); Zeiner (2007).
11. Cohen (2006, p. 537) and also Bell & Parchomovsky (2007); Garnett (2006); Serkin (2007).
12. Zeiner (2006, p. 531).
13. Mihaly (2007); Serkin (2007, p. 908).
14. Bell & Parchomovsky (2007); Kelly (2006); Benson (2005); Clauretie, Kuhn, & Schwer (2004); Garnett (2006).
15. Mihaly (2007, p. 27); see also Garnett (2006).
16. Benson (2005); Kelly (2006).
17. Cypher & Forgey (2003).
18. Esposto (1996).
19. Neimann & Shapiro (2008).
20. Serkin (2007).
21. Lopez & Totah (2007).
22. Calfee (2006).
23. Han (2008).
24. Knapp (2008).
25. Garnett (2006).
26. Farjad (2007).
27. Christensen (2005).
28. Wilder & Stigter (1989); Fawcett (1986).
29. Olejarski (2011a).
30. Olejarski (2011b).

Part III

PRAXIS: THEORY TO PRACTICE

Part III explores the relationships between takings theory and what it means to manage responsibly eminent domain in practice, given the use of administrative discretion. Through a balanced consideration of community members and practitioners' perspectives, empirical information is presented that may help to educate people actually involved in the implementation of eminent domain.

Chapter Five

Please Save the Neighborhood!

> *We really like this plan. I mean, who doesn't like trees and people and streetscapes and lattes. Croissants, for heaven sakes! This is great, this is good stuff, but please save the neighborhood.*
>
> —Amy Visciglia, Community member involved with *Kelo* takings

Up until this point, the book has focused on cultivating an understanding of the use of administrative discretion and the foundational issues and questions surrounding eminent domain. Now begins the exploration of eminent domain from the perspectives of those people actually involved with takings. This chapter shares the narrative of eminent domain in the 2005 *Kelo* case from the community members' perspective.

During interviews with public administrations throughout Connecticut, the birthplace of *Kelo*, many practitioners explained that the context of the situation plays an incredibly significant role in their decision-making process. An important part of the context of *Kelo* is the perspective of those community members closest to the case. In what should really be called a team effort, thanks to a number of people who participated in this research, I was able to interview extensively seven community members who were at the center of the *Kelo* controversy.

There was a small coalition of community organizers who came together to form the Coalition to Save Fort Trumbull Neighborhood. Within this group of grassroots activists, each member of the organization was responsible for a particular task. Kathleen Mitchell, longtime activist in New London, was charged with writing lead plaintiff Susette Kelo's speeches and releases. She is also the author of the famous Christmas card (picture included in chapter 1). Kathleen recently ran for Mayor of New London. Amy Visciglia and her husband, Steve Hallquist, were responsible for all legislative and policy activities. Susette Kelo put the "Kelo" in *Kelo v. New London*, and her husband is Timmy LeBlanc. And finally, Doug Schwartz was the neighborhood mailman. Susette described him as coming into neighbors' homes, making a sandwich, whether the resident was home or not, and then leaving the mail. It was a tight-knit community.[1]

My interview with Amy and Steve took place at their kitchen table one afternoon. I had been emailing Kathleen in the previous weeks because she was trying to convince Susette to let me interview her. At the end of one of my interviews with two public administrators earlier in the week, one retired judicial district chief clerk suggested that I stop by Amy and Steve's house, and gave me their address. I honestly had not planned to drop by, but something came over me, and I thought, "Why not? What's the worst that could happen?"

I knocked on the door, and Amy answered that she had heard about me and to come on in. At first, I was not sure if this was a good thing or not. She quickly calmed my nerves and told me that Kathleen had called to tell her that a graduate student researching eminent domain would probably be by to talk with her. Amy walked me up to her kitchen, and we sat at the table talking for hours. From the start, it was evident that she was quite knowledgeable about all of the technical, legislative nuances associated with the *Kelo* takings, something yet to be covered in any of the research I had read. So much that has been written on eminent domain in general and *Kelo* focuses on the legal precedents of the case or the fact that there was such a flurry of legislative activity in the wake of the case. But nothing really explained this case. And Amy was so balanced in her discussions with me, which will surely come through in the following sections of this chapter. Amy and I have had several follow-up phone conversations since our initial interview.

I was running late for a tour of the Fort Trumbull neighborhood, so Amy and I decided to meet up later that evening. After a whirlwind tour of the community, seeing mostly overgrown weeds and rocks and hearing about the neighborhood's newest residents, a crowd of feral cats, and meeting with Avner Gregory, the owner and part-time resident of the new site of the little pink house, I headed back to meet with Amy and Steve. After speaking for a bit with them, they needed to leave to pick up signs for a community event. Before leaving, however, Amy called Kathleen to ask if I could come meet with her. Kathleen agreed and asked if I could bring over some coffee filters.

It was a hot August night, sitting first at Kathleen's kitchen table and then later on her front porch, overlooking the river . . . and the new Pfizer facility. Kathleen was feisty in the most complimentary way; she called and *told*

Susette to come over to talk with me. She did promise her potato chips if she came over. After finishing up an ice-cream date-night, Susette and Timmy came to Kathleen's. At some point, Doug was walking by and came up to join in the conversation. Together we sat for over four hours on her front porch, eating chips and ice cream and drinking coffee. And lots of talking.

TRANSPARENCY

Most interesting about all of the interviews for this book is how similar the arguments on both sides are. Transparency was the major concern for the community members regarding the way the *Kelo* case was managed. But it was also the primary caution for the public administrators charged with making decisions surrounding eminent domain. Transparency of the eminent domain process really manifests itself in the form of education, particularly from the perspective of community members.

Transparency of the eminent domain process overall and, more specifically, the public hearings involved, is the main issue raised by the administrators that I interviewed and the people directly involved in the *Kelo* takings. Amy and Doug explained that the state funneled funds to the New London Development Corporation (NLDC) via the city of New London. Three state statutes were used in this case: Chapter 588l: Economic Development and Manufacturing Assistance (used for urban rehabilitation bonds); Chapter 130: Department of Economic and Community Development, Redevelopment and Urban Renewal (known as "the blight chapter"); and Chapter 132: Municipal Development Projects (used for economic development). Chapter 132 requires the city to designate a redevelopment agent, the NLDC, and also grants the authority for the NLDC to acquire property via eminent domain.

As Kathleen explained, "The state wouldn't give the city council the money [for the development] if they were going to manage it, so they had no choice but to reactivate the NLDC because the state wouldn't trust the city council with the money." Timmy added, "The state wouldn't trust them [the city] period." Kathleen expressed major concerns over this arrangement because the NLDC was made up almost entirely of people from other municipalities who were "making decisions for New London residents." She continued, "We couldn't vote them out of office." Timmy stated, "They [the NLDC] were all involved with politics, and they were just trying to make a dollar off New London's pocket. They didn't care what happened to the normal mom and pop." Steve described it as "a confluence of personalities."

This lack of accountability and transparency is significantly important in the implementation of eminent domain. What happened here is the state law required the local government of New London to grant the power to use eminent domain, on its behalf, to a quasi-public-private organization. This was problematic here because, as Kathleen aptly noted, citizens had no accountability check in place because they could not vote the NLDC members out of office. Members of Pfizer were on the NLDC. The strained relationship between the state, the city, and the hybrid organization made accountability more difficult, especially regarding public hearings required by state law.

I am going to wander for a moment to include some testimony from former Mayor of New London, Lloyd Beachy. This testimony was part of a public *hearing* of the state senate Planning and Development Committee. It was televised live on CT-N, Connecticut Network, on August 25, 2005, just two months after the Court's decision in *Kelo*.[2] During Beachy's testimony, he explained that one week after he became mayor, back in December of 1997, is when it all began.

Beachy had a two-hour meeting with the president of the NLDC, during which time she explained her "hopes and dreams for New London," using what Beachy described as the "big balloon chart" that included colored circles representing offices, parking, and homes in the new redevelopment site on Fort Trumbull. When he met at Pfizer's headquarters, three months later in February of 1998, the same "big balloon chart" was there. The problem, Beachy explained, was that this "grand ordained plan had pre-conceived plans." The city went through "what I call a sham," he continued.

Beachy's testimony included the role of the Connecticut Department of Economic and Community Development (DECD) in the New London eminent domain case. Regarding the DECD's "advisory assistance," Beachy stated: "I would love to be able to provide you with high stacks of minutes of meetings, but what I'm going to tell you about are the things that happen in those meetings where you don't take minutes." He continued, "This advisory assistance essentially was that every action the city council took was the result of paperwork that was presented to us principally by [DECD Deputy Commissioner]." Beachy persisted: "She [DECD Deputy Commissioner] would meet with council in executive session before our meetings and hand us resolutions that we were supposed to pass. We didn't have a chance to make any changes, in fact, we were told they weren't to be changed."

So Mayor Beachy requested a meeting with the DECD Commissioner. Beachy asked him, "What role does the city have to play in this development?" The commissioner replied, "Mr. Beachy, you have to understand, it's our money, we're gonna do what we want with it."

Beachy's testimony before the Planning and Development Committee concluded with the following:

> This is what happened in New London, CT. This was not a public process, it was a process that was stuffed down our throats by the state of Connecticut and some people who decided that they wanted to go for the money instead of taking care of our citizens. . . . We can do economic development in communities, as long as you don't do that [eminent domain]. It can be done by the private business agencies that wanna do business.

He was asked questions by senatorial members of the Planning and Development Committee regarding DECD's role in the planning process. The senators noted that they had trouble getting a straight answer from DECD and hoped Beachy could clarify: "What did they [DECD] actually come and tell you, directly or indirectly, as far as the details of what you were doing in your town." Beachy's response: "We were given the plan to approve. The plan was developed by NLDC with a number of consultants doing the work, and it went to the state for approval before we even saw it." When Beachy was asked about the types of resolutions the city was given by the DECD, he responded, "Virtually every one. For one resolution, DECD didn't even bother to cut the header off with the fax number with the name of the lobbyist who had drafted the legislation. This stuff was brought to us from Hartford [CT state capital]." He also noted, "There was no question that the funding was driving the decision" regarding the city council vote of 6-1, with Beachy as the 1, to approve the municipal redevelopment plan.

Beachy appeared to be a nice man with a sense of humor in an obviously trying time. The first (of two) senator to question him concluded by saying, "Thank you. It was worth the five and a half hours to hear you." Beachy, without missing a beat, replied, "Well, I've been waiting for five and a half years."

Susette, Kathleen, and Timmy all expressed serious concerns about the NLDC's tactics during the process of acquiring the properties needed for the development. Susette stated, "Nobody [in the neighborhood] wanted to move." To one family, Kathleen explained, "The NLDC was kind enough to allow them lifetime use of their house, so you know what they did? They dug up everything around it so it was just standing there." "Like a moat," Susette added. "And then they really couldn't stay there . . . because there was nothing to hold back the [rain] water and the basement was flooding," said Kathleen. Susette described a similar experience for another property owner, "They did the same thing to [another plaintiff]. They dug out all around [his] house, and they put Jersey barriers [concrete barriers frequently used as highway medians] up against his house. . . . His house was full of water." Susette continued to describe the ways in which the NLDC tried to intimidate property owners by calling social services on elderly residents, saying they were unfit to care for themselves, and calling the agency on another family, saying that the property was unfit for the child living in the home. Timmy and Susette also described NLDC officials driving through the neighborhood on a daily basis to intimidate property owners.

Susette noted, "What they did to us was wrong. It was wrong then, and it's still wrong now." "When all was said and done, it was pretty disgusting. It was just about as low as you could get," said Kathleen. Timmy added, "These NLDC people . . . these are very unscrupulous . . . very un-American people." Susette concluded, "Nobody in this country should have to live like we lived. Nobody. Like animals, like the wolves were at our doors for ten years. This is America, nobody should have to live that way."[3]

Lacking transparency of the process presented itself once again, this time regarding the designation of the Fort Trumbull neighborhood as blighted. According to Amy, "They [the city of New London] never designated it [the Fort Trumbull neighborhood] a blighted area. . . . We are a distressed community, but 'blighting' is something that has a statutory definition. That was their fatal error." She explained that this is what mobilized the community members' efforts in opposition to the NLDC's redevelopment efforts.

Related to the lack of blight designation is the empirical support provided by the city with regard to the neighborhood's poor condition. Recall in the discussion of the *Kelo* case that the Court cited the neighborhood's unemployment rate as being twice that of the state and that the population of the city declined to levels of the 1920s. Amy disputes the city's calculations, as cited in the case, particularly the high unemployment rate. She explained that the city included the naval center's closing, which resulted in a loss of about 1,500 jobs, in the unemployment rate, therefore inflating the number. Amy stated, "The little businesses that were there didn't lose employees. . . . It was an in-tact neighborhood" and continued listing and describing many of the specific neighborhood businesses that remained open and successful.

EDUCATION

Transparency also manifests in the form of education in the implementation of eminent domain proceedings. Transparency in the overall process is central to educating citizens and helping them to understand the process itself, as well as their role in it. Practitioners of public administration who participated in this study also stressed the importance of educating citizens as a mechanism to gain their support.

Both Doug and Amy explained how all three relevant Connecticut statutes require that the development plans receive formal approval prior to the initiation of eminent domain proceedings.[4] In order to receive formal approval, one public hearing is required. This discussion over a public *hearing*, compared with a public *meeting*, assumes a major role regarding issues of transparency of the takings process and public administrators' educating the public about the proceedings.

Residents of the Fort Trumbull neighborhood were supportive of improving the community when plans were first announced to redevelop the community. Amy explained her excitement: "I had a great hope for New London. I was excited." Amy and Steve attended what they were told were public *hearings* about the New London Development Corporation's (NLDC) redevelopment efforts for the community. They described the public's sentiment as being generally supportive of these efforts. She explained, "We really like this plan. I mean, who doesn't like trees and people and streetscapes and lattes. Croissants, for heaven sakes!"

What was somehow lost in translation, however, were community members' pleas to save the neighborhood. Amy added, "And we'd say, 'This is great, this is good stuff, but please save the neighborhood.'" Remember that the eminent domain process was described in chapter 1. Initiating eminent domain proceedings should be done as a last resort, according to the practitioners who participated in this study. Important here is striking a balance between new redevelopment efforts and maintaining the existing fabric of the community. This is what the community members were trying to express during what they were told were the public *hearings*. Community members involved in the coalition to save the neighborhood were not opposed to the city and the NLDC's redevelopment efforts holistically, but they were supportive of a plan that would incorporate the existing community into the plan. Amy also explained that after community members spoke at these hearings, a man would approach them. This man, she noted, would ask for the community members' names and address. The coalition discovered that he was a NLDC attorney.

These public *hearings* were not *hearings* but were rather public *meetings*. Although this distinction may appear to be merely linguistic nuance, it is significantly important from a legal and practical perspective.[5] State statutes require a public hearing in order for the NLDC's redevelopment plan of the Fort Trumbull neighborhood to be formally adopted. Moreover, the NDLC's ability to acquire properties for the development also hinges on formal approval of the plan.

Amy explained how the confusion between public hearings and public meetings began: "They [the NLDC] would say 'We're having a public meeting, we're having a public hearing,' and next thing you know, we're all calling them 'public hearings.' Those meetings, they weren't public hearings because public hearings have to have public officials there. They were there, but they weren't official." These public meetings were not official public hearings because the meetings were run by the NLDC officials, rather than the public officials on the city council.

This highlights the strained relationship between the NLDC and the city officials. More supporting evidence is found in newspaper articles from the local paper in New London, *The Day*. According to city employees, "During planning commission meetings, for example, Goebel [COO of NLDC] said his staff had tried to include city officials in the MDP [Municipal Development Plan] planning process, but that they 'just didn't show up.'" [6] The same article shows that planning officials from the city "strongly denied that they had been invited to the meeting." Another article quoted a city planning official stating, "Lack of communication is a problem. We can't attend meetings we weren't notified of."[7]

In January of 2000, the Planning and Zoning Commission held the one public *hearing* regarding the NLDC's redevelopment plan for the Fort Trumbull neighborhood. During this hearing, the New London city council voted to approve the plan. This action designated the NLDC as its development agent, therefore granting the NLDC the power of eminent domain to acquire property necessary for the plan's fulfillment.[8]

Amy described the meeting, which lasted about ten hours, she remembers. As the NLDC was advocating for approval of their redevelopment plan to the city council, New London residents found out why that NLDC lawyer had asked for their name and address during the previous public meetings. According to Amy, the NLDC argued, "We had six community meetings, and of those community meetings, 2,700 people stood up, or however many the number was, and said they liked the plan."

The importance of public administrators informing and educating citizens on their role in the eminent domain process is especially clear here. Amy explained: "The real fight started, but what we didn't know, sadly, was that the real place where we could insert ourselves in the process was over. We thought the fight was just getting warmed up, but it was a done deal." She continued, "No one broke the law, but no one informed us of what the law was of the process we were in." Note the distinction between legal and moral, enter administrative discretion. Amy explained: "We thought we were going to hearings, and we thought the information was going somewhere. We thought they were all hearings, and we didn't understand that 'hearing' was a legal term." Later in the year, the coalition members attempted to stop the properties that had already been taken by eminent domain from being demolished. According to a newspaper article, the city attorney's response was: "The time to protest demolition was in January when the City Council granted the power of eminent domain to the NLDC."[9]

During all of those public meetings that the community members attended, their message was clear: great plan, but please save the neighborhood. The lack of transparency went a long way in the *Kelo* takings in terms of alienating the community and failing to educate the citizens about the eminent domain process overall, and, most importantly, their role in the process. This is an especially important lesson for practitioners of public administration involved with takings regarding educating the public. Eminent domain already carries significant baggage with itself and often invokes distrust of government. Once eminent domain is put on the table, practitioners should learn from the *Kelo* case ways in which to genuinely educate and engage the public. It is particularly evident from this case that the community members were not opposed to the redevelopment plans for the neighborhood, in fact, it was just the opposite. More will be discussed on this in the next chapter on public administrators' understanding of eminent domain.

Image 5.1. Land where petitioners' property once stood. Source: Image by the author.

Image 5.2. Land where petitioners' property once stood; private men's club, Italian Dramatic Club. Source: Photo by the author.

Image 5.3. Land where petitioners' property once stood. Source: Photo by the author.

Image 5.4. Pfizer facility; land where petitioners' property once stood. Source: Photo by the author.

NOTES

1. The coalition's work is described in Benedict's (2009) work and also Olejarski & Webb Farley (2013) in greater detail.
2. Many thanks to New London, CT, community member Bob Stuller for sharing DVDs of the hearings with me.
3. Also in question is the timing of getting the redevelopment plan approved by the city council, the NLDC being designated as the city's redevelopment agent, and the acquiring of properties, all of which is explained in greater detail in Olejarski & Webb Farley (2013).
4. Chapter 588l (§32–224 *et seq.*); Chapter 130 (§8–127 *et seq.*); Chapter 132 (§8–192 *et seq.*; §8–193 *et seq.*).
5. Luckily, the CT-N broadcast of the Planning and Development Committee public *hearing* with Mayor Beachy's testimony was clearly labeled as a hearing.
6. "Fort Trumbull plan approved" (2000).
7. "City agencies back NLDC" (2000).
8. "Councilors say they agonize" (2000).
9. "Petition seeking vote" (2000).

Chapter Six

Administrative Discretion in Action

It's [eminent domain] such a highly controversial activity. . . . It has such a high visibility factor . . . people live and die off of it politically, administratively, and otherwise.

—A Connecticut Town Manager

In this chapter, administrators' perceptions and understanding of eminent domain is explored. This helps to pull together a more complete picture of public administration in action. The focus is on administrative discretion in the decision-making process. Administrative discretion is informal authority that practitioners exercise when they participate in the policy-making process; by making decisions about their understanding and interpretations of vague policies, they assume an active role in the process. Discretion *should* be a value-based balancing of the administrators' professionalism (expertise, competency, development and training, and experience) and ethics and a reflection of the community, the idea of being responsible and responsive.

ADMINISTRATORS' PROFESSIONALISM AND UNDERSTANDING OF EMINENT DOMAIN

Before we can delve deeply into an exploration of how public administrators use their discretion in the eminent domain process, it is important to develop a foundational grounding on their professionalism and perception of takings. Here, the notion of professionalism is inclusive of practitioners' knowledge of issues relating to eminent domain, such as their familiarity with *Kelo* and local ordinances and state statutes affecting takings in their communities.

This section also explores administrators' understanding of the ways *Kelo*, as a landmark eminent domain ruling, has affected their perceptions of takings.

The following analysis of administrators' understanding of eminent domain is the result of a small survey that was sent to Connecticut administrators, practitioners and elected officials, mostly at the local level. It is intended to provide an overview of administrators' perceptions and understanding; more importantly, the survey was intended to provide a starting point for the more in-depth interview analyses that follow. Therefore, the data in Tables 6.1 and 6.2 are presented briefly and in a straightforward way.

From the results of the survey of Connecticut administrators, analysis shows that they reported being most familiar with local ordinances relating to eminent domain, followed by the *Kelo* case, state statutes affecting takings, and, finally, the Takings Clause of the U.S. Constitution, which grants the takings power. As the birthplace of *Kelo*, it is not surprising that over half of the practitioners surveyed reported being very familiar with the case (54 percent). This is especially important because it shows that administrators are aware of and familiar with the case, which should help to paint a fuller picture about their perceptions and understanding of the case's impact on eminent domain in local government. Most importantly, however, is the strong percentage of administrators that reported being very familiar with local ordinances (48 percent) and state statutes affecting eminent domain (39 percent). This shows that practitioners who participated in this research are quite knowledgeable about the big-picture state policies and local ordinances that govern takings in their government.

Although practitioners reported being very familiar with *Kelo*, these survey results show that administrators are far less familiar with the precedent cases in *Kelo* that were discussed earlier in this book. This may be somewhat of a concern, as few practitioners are familiar with the established doctrines on which the *Kelo* decision was based. It appears that practitioners' familiarity shows mixed results, with administrators being knowledgeable about the landmark case but not with the historical foundations and, more importantly, the evolution of issues and questions surrounding the controversy.

Regarding administrators' experience with eminent domain, only ten percent of survey participants reported having very frequent professional takings experience. This finding should be viewed cumulatively with administrators' familiarity with relevant local ordinances and state statutes, which show a much higher knowledge than formal professional experience with eminent domain. This has to do with practitioners' explaining that eminent domain should only be used as a last resort, when all pre-condemnation strategies have provided infeasible.

Table 6.1. Administrators' Professionalism

Administrators' Professionalism	Response Option Percentages						
Familiarity with							
Kelo	6%	8%	16%	15%	22%	32%	Not at all – Very familiar
Local ordinance(s)	15%	7%	18%	10%	13%	35%	Not at all – Very familiar
State statute(s)	11%	15%	16%	18%	19%	20%	Not at all – Very familiar
Takings Clause	17%	20%	12%	19%	18%	13%	Not at all – Very familiar
Familiarity with precedent cases in Kelo	37%	25%	16%	7%	4%	8%	Not at all – Very familiar
Applicability of Takings Clause to eminent domain	11%	12%	17%	12%	8%	30%	Not at all – Very applicable
Eminent domain experience							
Professionally	43%	25%	11%	11%	4%	6%	Not at all – Very frequently
Personally	87%	6%	1%	3%	0%	0%	Not at all – Very frequently
Contracting out with private firms	44%	25%	6%	4%	1%	3%	Not at all – Very frequently

Table 6.2. Administrators' Understanding

ADMINISTRATORS' UNDERSTANDING						
	Response Option Percentages					
Kelo's *impact on eminent domain*	37% (Not at all)	15%	6%	6%	4%	14% (Very significant)
Kelo's *impact on*						
Number of takings	58% (Not at all)	4%	2%	4%	4%	8% (Very significant)
Pre-condemnation strategies	46% (Not at all)	10%	4%	4%	4%	8% (Very significant)
Contracting out	56% (Not at all)	8%	1%	3%	2%	4% (Very significant)
Kelo *changed*	No change	Decreased	Increased			
Number of takings	75%	10%	1%			
Pre-condemnation strategies	61%	5%	11%			
Contracting out	67%	1%	4%			
Agree						
ED in general	8% (Not at all)	23%	21%	14%	14%	15% (Strongly agree)
Kelo	28% (Not at all)	23%	19%	8%	8%	8% (Strongly agree)
ED for private development	51% (Not at all)	25%	12%	6%	1%	1% (Strongly agree)
ED for economic development	23% (Not at all)	22%	20%	14%	11%	4% (Strongly agree)
Understand						
Eminent domain	0% (Not at all)	6%	16%	19%	27%	29% (Very well)
Kelo	4% (Not at all)	13%	22%	15%	25%	19% (Very well)

These survey results in Table 6.2 show how Connecticut administrators who participated in this research understand *Kelo*'s impact on takings. Practitioners responded that the most recent landmark case on eminent domain had a moderate impact, with one-fifth noting that *Kelo* had a very significant affect. Just over half (52 percent) responded that the case had very little impact.

When reviewing the data on *Kelo*'s impact on the number of takings, localities' use of pre-condemnation strategies, and contracting out with private firms on issues relating to eminent domain, more findings begin to emerge. Over ten percent of practitioners reported that the case had a very significant impact on the number of takings, and the data also show that this came in the form of a strong decrease in the number of takings. Further, administrators' responses show that *Kelo* very significantly impacted their locality's use of pre-condemnation strategies by way of strongly increasing such strategies. This shows that the idea of using eminent domain as a last resort for municipal projects is a strong value in local government in Connecticut. There also appears to be some movement regarding local governments' increasing use of contracting out issues relating to takings with private firms post-*Kelo*. As with many small local governments, municipalities contract out with private firms on an as-needed basis, rather than consistently employ someone through the local government, largely to do cost-saving efforts.

Now, here is where the survey results get *really* interesting. When asked about their general agreement with eminent domain, almost one-third (29 percent) of practitioners reported strong agreement and just about one-third (31 percent) reported disagreement, with the remaining forty percent falling somewhere in between. When asked about agreement with the *Kelo* case, over half (51 percent) of the practitioners reported disagreement, with about one-fifth (16 percent) reporting strong agreement.

In *Kelo*, the central question causing all the controversy was whether eminent domain could be used for economic development. These results show that almost half (45 percent) of practitioners surveyed disagree with economic development takings. More importantly, however, is that three-quarters (76 percent) of administrators disagree with eminent domain being used for private development, with only two percent in strong agreement.

All of this is to say that these data show that practitioners in the home state of *Kelo* generally agree with the use of eminent domain, as it is a powerful tool for local governments to use in advancement of the public good. Nearly all administrators, however, disagree with using takings for private gain, which has been a major concern for the general public in a post-*Kelo* environment. It also appears to be a strong indicator that economic development will continue to be a controversial use of eminent domain, as about half of the practitioners surveyed disagree. Administrators' understanding of eminent domain in general (56 percent) and the *Kelo* case (44 percent) shows that just about half of the practitioners reported understanding each very well. This helps to understand their perceptions of takings and the case, as fewer than ten percent reported not understanding eminent domain well.

ADMINISTRATIVE DISCRETION IN ACTION

Now that we have examined practitioners' professionalism and understanding of eminent domain, focus shifts to exploring public administration in action: discretion. This section looks at relationships between practitioners' professionalism and understanding and how that manifests as their use of administrative discretion. Here, the in-depth interviews with public administrators' prove to be very insightful in understanding discretion in the takings process.

Reviewing the data in Table 6.3 helps to provide a more comprehensive picture of administrators' use of discretion in the context of eminent domain.[1] These survey results show what factors, professionalism (e.g., familiarity with *Kelo*, local ordinances and state statutes affecting eminent domain, the Takings Clause, and also professional experience), are contributing to the development of practitioners' understanding. These relationships show administrators' discretion in action.

These survey results show that practitioners' professional experience with takings appears to have a moderate influence on their understanding of *Kelo*'s impact on the use of eminent domain (16.8 percent), the number of takings (17.7 percent), and the use of pre-condemnation strategies (16.6 percent). In other words, administrators' who participated in this research reported that the more professional experience they had with eminent domain, the more likely he or is was to view *Kelo* as having a stronger impact on takings in the community. It is also interesting to see what factors influence practitioners' perceptions of *Kelo*'s impact on contracting out with private firms for issues relating to eminent domain. Here, there are negative relationships, meaning that greater practitioner familiarity with *Kelo* (–19.6 percent) and local takings-related ordinances (–15.3 percent) result in a decrease in the use of private firms. This makes sense because a practitioner having greater familiarity should have less of a need to contract with an outside, private firm, since the knowledge is possessed in-house within the government.

Open-ended survey responses show that administrators' would be most likely to contract out with private legal, redevelopment or economic development, or real estate development firms. Administrators noted that legal firms would be retained to assist with the drafting of local ordinances, litigation, clarifying relevant laws, and preparing for eminent domain

Table 6.3. Administrative Discretion in Action[1]

Administrative Discretion in Action					
	Familiarity with *Kelo*	Familiarity with Local Ordinance(s)	Familiarity with State Statute(s)	Familiarity with Takings Clause	Professional Experience with Eminent Domain
Kelo's impact on eminent domain					16.8%**
Kelo's impact on number of takings					17.1%**
Kelo's impact on pre-condemnation strategies					16.6%**
Kelo's impact on contracting out	-19.6%**	-15.3%**			
Agree with eminent domain in general	26.0%***		25.9%***		27.6%***
Agree with *Kelo*	17.2%**		20.8%**		
Agree with eminent domain for private development			14.1%**		
Agree with eminent domain for economic development	18.8%**		34.8%***	24.1%***	32.5%***
Understand eminent domain	38.0%***	34.9%***	42.0%***	38.0%***	38.8%***
Understand *Kelo*	60.2%***	25.1%***	38.9%***	43.2%***	38.8%***

1. The statistical measure of association employed is Somers' d. This measure was used because it is an asymmetrical measure of association, as well as a proportionate reduction in error (PRE) statistic, which means that it provides support for a causal relationship, in addition to helping to reduce the error in predicting the value of the dependent variable dimension. Figures shown are for the percentages, which show the strength and direction of the relationship between practitioners' knowledge and experience (columns) and practitioners' understanding (rows). Asterisks are used to indicate the significance levels of the relationships: * significant at 0.1 (10% likely to occur by chance), **significant at 0.05 (5% likely to occur by chance), *** significant at 0.01 (1% likely to occur by chance).

proceedings. Other external firms may be hired to conduct a study about a potential project, develop a long-range development plan, provide direction to the elected body, provide support for the need for the taking, or to defer the use of eminent domain. Outside real estate firms were frequently noted as being hired to assist with property valuation or assessment, as noted in both the survey and interviews.

With regard to post-*Kelo* impact on the use of pre-condemnation strategies, the open-ended survey responses provide a good deal of insight with regard to the steps administrators are taking before initiating eminent domain proceedings. On one hand, these strategies included not taking a residential home "under any circumstance," implementing a "more rigorous blight ordinance," negotiating partnership strategies with property owners, reducing the number of properties necessary for projects, expanded compensation packages (e.g., beyond market value or relocation assistance), and increased discussion. Alternatively, though in the minority, several administrators described a heightened emphasis on "increase to tax base," "extensive use of partial takings," and using "takings that do not require a premium over market value" (i.e., this administrator noted that redevelopment takings require compensation of 110 percent of market value).

Administrators with more professional eminent domain experience responded that *Kelo* significantly impacted their municipality's use of pre-condemnation strategies. Combined with the fact that 11 percent of survey respondents indicated that they had increased the use of pre-condemnation strategies after *Kelo*, this suggests that post-*Kelo*, municipalities are engaging in the use of pre-condemnation strategies to avoid using eminent domain more frequently. This finding was the most strongly supported among interview participants overall, regardless of their level of agreement with eminent domain. Responses ranged from a planner's "negotiate, don't take," a zoning board of appeals chairman's statement that their role is to be "master planners . . . to work and redesign plans to avoid using eminent domain," a town manager's need to "justify that no other alternative" exists but to use eminent domain, and a selectman's need for an "absolute emergency" to use eminent domain. During an interview with a land use attorney and a redevelopment director, they described an increase in the use of partial takings or land swaps. In their experience with takings, 80 percent result in "friendly purchases," with only about 1 percent of the remaining 20 percent actually going to trial. One development director explained that the municipality tries to use tax liens or foreclosures to take properties instead of using eminent domain.

Based on the interview participants' responses, the two largest pre-condemnation strategies employed by Connecticut administrators are using zoning variances, special permits, and alternative development plans, as well as pre-condemnation negotiations with property owners over the amount of compensation to be provided for the taking of private property. The latter was discussed far more during the interviews. One town manager described this as "pay[ing] for goodwill before [using] eminent domain." The chair of a land use commission described the success of pre-condemnation negotiations as being largely dependent on whether the parties involved on the part of the government "know how to negotiate" and that eminent domain would only be used if "someone [was] being unreasonable" or "hold[ing] up progress," according to a selectman who also holds an administrative appointment in a second municipality. One administrator who is a councilman in one municipality and a planner in another described eminent domain as a "right" that governments do not always have to use.

The perspective shared by most administrators who participated in the interviews was that pre-condemnation negotiations amount to a balancing of the cost to the public, with regard to just compensation, and the cost to the property owner for the loss during the taking. Described frequently was the actual negotiation process, which involves outlining to the property owner that the government is willing to pay a certain amount in just compensation, but that if the case were to be litigated, the additional costs to the community would be another certain amount. Rather than pay these additional costs in litigation, the practitioners explained that they would prefer to pass along the additional funds to the property owner in the compensation package. Under this framework, not only is the property owner more fairly compensated, but the community at large is also more supportive of the project requiring the taking because they know that the property owners have been compensated in such a manner, instead of the municipality spending the resources on litigation. As one development director asked, "How do you do a public good at a reasonable price?"

As explained by an assessor, pre-condemnation negotiations generally require five appraisals from the government and the property owner. All appraisals must conform to the standards set forth by Uniform Standards of Professional Appraisal Practice, which "guards against pre-determined valu[ations]." These appraisals then serve as the basis for the compensation package offered to the property owner. A representative town meeting official noted that "fair market-value and fair market-worth are two separate things." Key to the negotiation strategy is designing a compensation package that approaches, if not meets, the worth of the property to the owner to avoid using eminent domain.

Practitioners' understanding, with regard to their overall agreement with eminent domain in general, shows that it is moderately associated with their knowledge of *Kelo* (26.0 percent) and state statutes relevant to eminent domain

(25.9 percent), as well as professional experience (27.6 percent). Here, the survey results show that more knowledgeable practitioners reported being more likely to agree with takings. This was also the case that administrators with more professional experience were more likely to agree with eminent domain.

Agreement with *Kelo* shows moderate to moderately strong relationships with practitioners' knowledge and familiarity with the case (17.2 percent) and state statutes (20.8 percent). Regarding practitioners' agreement with eminent domain for private development, only their knowledge of relevant state statutes (14.1 percent) indicates that a moderate relationship exists. Finally, practitioners' agreement with eminent domain for economic development shows that a range of relationships exist. For example, knowledge and familiarity with *Kelo* influences administrators' reported agreement in a moderate way (18.8 percent), as is also the case with the Takings Clause (24.1 percent). Practitioners' knowledge of state statutes, however, shows a strong relationship, or that administrators with more knowledge of these relevant statutes (34.8 percent) are more likely to support economic development takings. Professional experience appears to influence strongly administrators' agreement (32.5 percent).

Overall, practitioners with the highest degree of familiarity or the most previous professional experience with eminent domain are the most likely to strongly agree with each of the four eminent domain dimensions (takings in general, *Kelo*, takings for private development, and takings for economic development). This means that those administrators with more experience or familiarity are more likely to agree than those with minimal familiarity or lacking experience. This does not, however, mean that the administrators with high familiarity and frequent experience always agree, particularly with eminent domain for private development. Survey respondents indicated the strongest agreement with eminent domain in general, followed by economic development, *Kelo*, and private development, with little agreement for the latter. This blends to provide support for the assertion that practitioners generally agree with eminent domain overall, as well as for economic development, and that those administrators who have the highest levels of professional experience or familiarity with relevant eminent domain statutes overwhelmingly support these uses in particular. These findings suggest that practitioners with professional experience and a self-reported familiarity understand that eminent domain is a powerful tool that is to be used cautiously and responsibly.

Practitioners' understanding of and subsequent agreement with eminent domain in general and for economic and private development proved to be the most divisive topic addressed during the interviews. Figure 6.1 below shows a typology of administrators' discretion with eminent domain that emerged from the interviews. During the interviews, two major issues as-

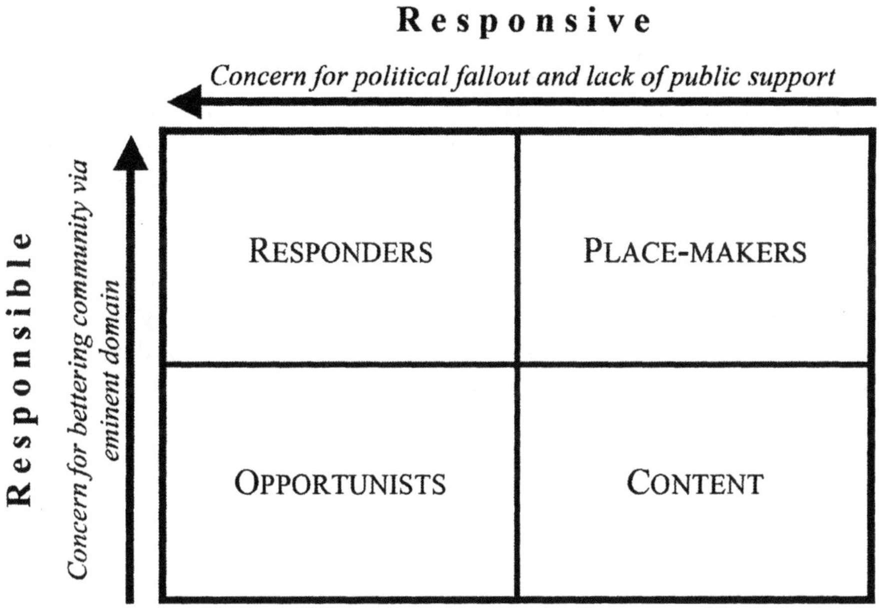

Figure 6.1. A Typology of Administrators' Discretion

sociated with the use of eminent domain emerged: practitioners' concern for political fallout and lack of public support and concern for bettering the community via the use of eminent domain.

This four-part typology of administrators' discretion in the context of eminent domain is the result of quite an organic process. I was hoping to uncover an understanding of issues relating to political fallout and lack of public support, or political v. legal authority to use eminent domain, during the interview phase of this research. I asked administrators participating in the interview questions surrounding how they would respond to a municipal development plan involving minimal public support, what factors would contribute to their final decision, and how they would go about the process of learning more about the project and the perspectives of the stakeholders involved. As I continued interviewing administrators, themes began to emerge regarding these issues, which I continued pursuing throughout the interview phase of the project. Though my intention was not to develop such a typology, the themes ultimately led to the development of one through this iterative process.

Figure 6.1, therefore, includes the categorization of four types of administrators based on their use of discretion, with regard to the implementation of eminent domain, in the context of political fallout and a broad community welfare. Factors also contributing to these two dimensions include the type of municipality (i.e., urban or rural) and subsequent economic conditions affecting the community, as well as historical uses of eminent domain at the municipal, state, and federal levels. These four categories include responders, place-makers, opportunists, and content administrators.[2] Place-makers are by far the rarest category of administrators' understanding of eminent domain, and opportunists are more common.

Practitioners who are categorized as *place-makers* make decisions regarding the use of eminent domain based predominantly on a high degree of concern for the bettering of the community and a relatively low degree of concern for political fallout and lack of public support for development projects. Place-makers are generally found in urban communities with a scarcity of available land to develop. Administrators in these municipalities typically engage quite frequently in the use of eminent domain or pre-condemnation negotiations. These practitioners are more aggressive, not in the pejorative sense, but rather, by seeking out development opportunities and using creative strategies, such as partial takings and private funding sources, to develop projects that will benefit the broader community. Particularly important to place-makers is the need to involve actively the public in the process, relying on community hearings to build support. In the absence of such support, place-makers reported that they would still be likely to initiate a development plan that could potentially involve the use of eminent domain if they believed it would improve the community. One place-maker called this "shaping the community in the public interest." Because place-makers have a strong history of community involvement and transparency, the public is generally more supportive of plans they bring forth. Further, because they use outside-the-box strategies and negotiations, they are able to provide more compensation, both monetary and alternative solutions, therefore lending more public support.

Practitioners who may be categorized as *responders* have both a high degree of concern for political fallout and lack of public support and concern for bettering the community via the use of eminent domain. Like place-makers, responders are typically found in urban communities, therefore increasing the need to use eminent domain or pre-condemnation negotiations to acquire properties necessary for development plans. Responders use eminent domain frequently, but not to the extent of place-makers. This is due to their heightened concern for political fallout and lacking public support for such projects. Key to the responder category of administrators is that they respond to the will of the public, both in terms of initiating projects and in deciding not to continue with a project that lacks support. Unlike place-makers' municipalities, responders' municipalities have a history of eminent domain that affects contemporary development projects. Several responders referred to redevelopment during the 1950s and 60s as "negro removal" because of the frequent toll on marginalized, minority populations. As a result, eminent domain still remains a difficult subject, as the public and administrators have a long memory of state and federal redevelopment projects of the past. Because responders engage in eminent domain and pre-condemnation negotiations resulting from strong public support for a particular development project, they are more limited than place-makers in their ability to provide creative compensation packages (i.e., fewer private funding resources). Still, however, responders do make creative attempts when public support allows.

Practitioners in the *opportunists* category make decisions related to the potential use of eminent domain based on a high degree of concern for political fallout and lack of public support and a low degree of concern for bettering the community. These administrators are generally found in more rural communities with a good amount of available land to develop. Here, these administrators are much more concerned with political fallout and lacking public support for reasons similar to responders. Opportunists, however, are part of communities with an even stronger fear of state and federal eminent domain intervention, resulting from redevelopment projects, brownfields contamination sites, and highway construction (i.e., Interstate 95). Many of these administrators and their communities remain resentful, not in an irrational manner, of the ways in which highways were constructed, and the subsequent affects on communities, in prior decades and are unlikely to engage in projects that could potentially involve the use of eminent domain. The opportunists are quite similar to responders, yet they differ in the degree to which they are concerned with political fallout, with the former being much more extreme. As a result, this concern trumps a concern to better the community, so these administrators rarely engage in the use of eminent domain or pre-condemnation negotiations. The conditions under which they would do so would involve overwhelming public support and would almost never include private development. Affects of past eminent domain-related issues have shaped these administrators and their communities to value strongly individual rights and private property protections. This situation leads opportunists to engage in development plans much more passively than any other category and generally do so when an opportunity presents itself, rather than seeking out opportunities.

Finally, practitioners that may be categorized as being *content* have low degrees of concern for political fallout and lacking public support and concern for bettering the community. These administrators are typically found in rural communities, and content administrators' municipalities generally have substantial land available to develop or government-owned land. One content administrator noted that the municipality had upwards of 50 percent of the land available. Content administrators rarely engage in development projects, whether they could potentially involve the use of eminent domain or not. While they are concerned about political fallout to some degree, the municipality's lack of historically using eminent domain and a history absent state or federal intervention has not affected their community in the ways of the other categories. Further, content practitioners and their communities are generally, well, content with the state of their municipality and do not seek out opportunities for change.

Given that the major controversy in *Kelo* was the government's taking of private property to turn over to another private owner for development, these findings suggest that property owners, public administrators, and academics concerned with the erosion of the public use requirement of the Takings Clause should find some solace in knowing that administrators charged with implementing eminent domain policies generally do not agree with eminent domain for private development. When they do employ their power of eminent domain for private development, however, they do so with a strong regard for the welfare of the community.

This means that further efforts to study eminent domain would be well-advised to employ the case-study methodology. Much has been learned about the ways in which practitioners understand eminent domain in this study. Since administrators who responded to the survey generally indicated a low level of professional experience with eminent domain, disseminating the findings of case-study research may be able to serve as a substitute for the lack of this real-world experience or to bolster minimal experience.

Because the practitioners who participated in this study were closest to *Kelo* and reported high levels of familiarity with the case and following it in the local news, they were in quite a knowledgeable position to evaluate the case. As administrators in other states did not have the advantage of being highly exposed to relevant information, they likely lack a heightened awareness of the key issues and lessons learned by the case. Scholarly inquiries in the form of case studies may help to increase other administrators' awareness and understanding, as well as to learn subsequently from the perspectives and behaviors of practitioners with eminent domain experience.

Practitioners' responses regarding their understanding of eminent domain in general, as well as of the *Kelo* case, produce some strong relationship with their knowledge and professional experience with eminent domain. Perceptions of eminent domain is most strongly related to knowledge of state statutes (42.0 percent), followed closely by professional experience (38.8 percent), knowledge of *Kelo* (38.0 percent), the Takings Clause (38.0 percent), and, finally, local ordinances relevant to takings (34.9 percent). What this shows is that how administrators understand eminent domain is strongly influenced by all of these factors, meaning that how knowledgeable a practitioner reported being, strengthened by professional experience, all contribute to developing administrators' understanding of eminent domain.[3]

Likewise, administrators' understanding of *Kelo* is strongly influenced by their knowledge and experience. The strong relationship, not surprisingly, is with familiarity with the case (60.2 percent). Knowledge of the Takings Clause (43.2 percent), state eminent domain statutes (38.9 percent), professional experience (38.8 percent), and local ordinances (25.1 percent) follow. Once again, the more knowledgeable practitioners reported being, the more likely they were to report a strong understanding of the *Kelo* case.

These findings have several implications. First, practitioners' familiarity and understanding is likely affected by some degree of inflation, coupled with a much stronger reliance on self-guided efforts to increase familiarity. According to a town manager who participated in an interview, administrators report understanding eminent domain so well "because it's such a highly controversial activity. . . . It has such a high visibility factor . . . people live and die off of it politically, administratively, and otherwise."

Second, interviews revealed that practitioners generally did not follow the case in the media coverage from the beginning but sought further information once the case approached the U.S. Supreme Court. Therefore, once it became evident that *Kelo* presented something with which administrators should be concerned or aware, they took action. It was quite surprising during the interviews to hear a general sense of disbelief each time the case progressed up through the court system. Because a number of interview participants described minimal interest in the case during the early stages, it appears that much of their familiarity results from the case's arrival to the Supreme Court. With regard to their familiarity with eminent domain more broadly, however, the interviews revealed that they were familiar with other instances of eminent domain in neighboring municipalities throughout the state.

Further, and this is especially important, practitioners who participated in the interviews responded that they had experience with the process leading up to eminent domain (i.e., pre-condemnation strategies to avoid using eminent domain), in addition to direct experience with eminent domain. Perhaps some of the misleading survey results are due to the confines of the survey instrument used; future research would do well to consider broadening the language to include pre-condemnation negotiations and discussions of potentially using eminent domain.

When a practitioners' municipality, or a neighboring municipality, was faced with an issue related to eminent domain, the administrators reported seeking out the relevant ordinances and statutes for more information. During the interviews, administrators often referred to such issues as the impetus for their search for guidance and subsequent familiarity and understanding of eminent domain. In addition, administrators responded that their familiarity and understanding were shaped by resources external to the municipality, such as books, newspaper articles, the media, the internet, professional organizations, and other experiences they had with municipal boards, commissions, and committees.

Post-*Kelo*, a number of practitioners who participated in the interviews were responsible for crafting local ordinances. One representative town meeting official explained that the municipality sought out the post-*Kelo* eminent domain ordinance of a neighboring community for more information. Another land use commission administrator reported searching for academic and non-academic articles on the internet for clarification on the key issues of the case. Therefore, administrators' knowledge was shaped and informed by broader resources.

Insight into how well practitioners understand eminent domain as it relates to their previous professional experience is quite a significant finding. Certainly, the survey results indicate that the more frequently an administrator engages in eminent domain professionally, the more likely he is to understand it very well. Speaking to the complexity of issues related to eminent domain, however, is the fact that administrators with little to no professional eminent domain experience also responded that they understood eminent domain very well.

This relationship was quite dichotomous, with high percentages of administrators' understanding eminent domain very well at either end of the professional experience continuum. From the interviews, this finding appears to be related to administrators' knowledge with eminent domain. Although practitioners may not have substantial professional experience with eminent domain, many interview participants described experience with the takings process. This experience was in the context of discussing the possibility of using eminent domain for a particular project or in the pre-condemnation process. Further, the use or potential use of eminent domain in other municipalities throughout the state frequently prompted administrators' to seek out more information about the relevant issues in order to have a better understanding.

Another possible explanation of the finding is the way in which administrators perceive of their understanding of eminent domain. The interviews revealed that practitioners were, overall, quite knowledgeable about issues related to eminent domain and often had strong opinions. Administrators who had substantial professional eminent domain experience, however, possessed a different level of understanding. As one planner described it, there are different types of understanding in terms of "the process. . . the concept. . . [and] from a completely legal perspective."

Implicit in the typology of practitioners' understanding in Figure 6.1 is the role of administrators' professional experience with eminent domain. Practitioners categorized as place-makers and responders had more substantial professional experience with takings. These administrators also expressed more understanding about the balance between being concerned with political fallout and lacking public support and being concerned with bettering the community through development projects that could potentially involve the use of eminent domain.

Following this chapter on practitioners' use of discretion with the implementation of eminent domain is the exploration of their search for guidance during the takings process. Administrators' guidance search on issues relating to eminent domain should also be useful for interested community members, as they may want to consider using these resources, as well. These findings should be of interest for scholars and students of public administration because of their comprehensive nature and deep analysis as an entrée into the study of eminent domain from the perspective of praxis.

NOTES

1. Pollock (2005) provides a helpful guide for interpreting the strength of a PRE statistic. For relationships in which the percentage of the statistical measure of association is less than 10 percent, the relationship is weak; relationships between 11 and 20 percent are moderate; relationships between 21 and 30 percent are moderately strong; and relationships greater than 30 percent are strong. He also notes that PRE statistical measures of association indicating a relationship greater than 50 percent are uncommon in social science data, particularly for individual-level survey data.
2. "Content" as in the adjective of general satisfaction, rather than the noun meaning of contain.
3. Evaluating administrators' self-reported level of understanding of eminent domain and *Kelo* should be exercised cautiously in order to minimize socially desirable responses and inflated results. This was alleviated to the extent possible in the survey by including these questions in the latter half of the instrument to enable administrators participating in the survey to consider their understanding as they responded to the variety of previous questions.

Chapter Seven

Lost and Found: Administrators' Search for Guidance

It doesn't always matter if the public doesn't agree . . . The average citizen didn't know what the city was doing.

—A Connecticut Town Planner

Responsibly managing issues and questions surrounding eminent domain involves deeper exploration of administrative discretion. In this chapter, practitioners' search for eminent domain guidance is covered to bring forth their decision-making process and the resources they engage when looking for takings information. Community members and other interested scholars and students would do well to consider also these resources when faced with eminent domain questions.

ADMINISTRATORS' SEARCH FOR EMINENT DOMAIN GUIDANCE

Given the overwhelming lack of scholarship on the subject, discussing where administrators are likely to turn is an appropriate step in building the body of empirical knowledge on administrators' search for guidance. Administrators' search for eminent domain is quite complex, as practitioners appear to either be very likely or not at all likely to turn to each source for guidance. See Table 7.1 below for where Connecticut administrators are likely to turn for eminent domain guidance.

Administrators who participated in this study were very likely to turn to state statutes affecting eminent domain for guidance (69.0 percent), followed by local ordinances (54.0 percent), state Supreme Court decisions (49.0 percent),

Table 7.1. Administrators' Search for Eminent Domain Guidance[1]

Administrators' Search for Eminent Domain Guidance		
Variable	Percent Very Likely[2]	Percent Very Unlikely
State ED statute(s)	69	7
Local ED ordinance(s)	54	20
State Supreme Court decisions	49	18
Property owner's perspective	42	22
State Constitution	38	29
US Supreme Court decisions	36	29
Peers or colleagues	32	26
Municipal administrator	31	33
Municipal elected official	30	34
US Constitution	30	36
Professional experience	26	48
Professional organizations	26	32
State elected official	24	39
Professional conferences	22	40
Neighboring municipalities	22	27
Law review articles	19	47
State administrator	16	48
Academic journal articles	16	58
Direct supervisor	15	62
JD administrator	14	61
Community organizations	14	46
Interest groups	13	54
Neighboring JDs	11	51
Colleges or universities	11	63
Personal experience	10	74
Family or friends	10	66
Local newspapers	9	58
Local media	9	66
Neighboring states	8	62
National newspapers	7	65
National media	4	73

1. See Appendix B for expanded data on administrators' search for eminent domain guidance, including median, mode, and mean.
2. These percentages are based on the total number of survey responses for each question. The left column includes response options of 5 to 6 to show the highest likelihood; the right column includes response options of 1 to 2 to show the lowest likelihood.

property owner's perspective (42.0 percent), state Constitution (38.0 percent), and U.S. Supreme Court decisions (36.0 percent). From a normative perspective, it is a major finding of this study that the property owner's perspective is highly valued by practitioners in their search for guidance, with 42.0 percent of administrators responding that they are very likely to consider it. This relates strongly to the findings in the previous chapter regarding the typology of administrators' discretion and the dynamics of being responsive and responsible. Plus, this is good news for the constitutionalist perspective in public administration, regarding the rule of law as the foundation of the governance process, that practitioners rely heavily on U.S. Supreme Court decisions.

Administrators responded that they were twice as likely to turn to peers or colleagues (32.0 percent) than they were to turn to their direct supervisor (15.0 percent). This finding speaks strongly to the role of administrative discretion in the process of implementing eminent domain in that practitioners are much more likely to turn to fellow administrators with similar levels of experience and responsibilities, rather than those with a supervisory capacity. These practitioners appear to be exercising strongly their informal authority.

Turning equally to municipal administrators (31.0 percent) and municipal elected officials (31.0 percent) in their search for guidance is likely a result of the role of the municipal attorney in the process of implementing eminent domain. The equality of reliance on administrators and elected officials provides support for the lack of a politics-administration dichotomy at the local-government level and the more appropriate all-hands-on-deck environment. One interview participant, a town manager, described the relationship between elected officials and "professional administrators" as being one of reliance. Because elected officials are generally part-time, they rely heavily on practitioners for guidance. He also noted, however, the strong presence of political agendas in the process, particularly in situations involving partisan legislative bodies.

Following is administrators' likelihood to turn to their previous professional experience (26.0 percent) for eminent domain guidance. This suggests that practitioners are complementing their previous professional experience with other resources, such as those discussed above. Also, one town manager explained that he and his staff try to "get ahead" of issues before they become significant; it appears that for situations unfamiliar to administrators, previous experience may not provide the most guidance.

Public administrators participating in the research for this book responded that they were very likely to turn to neighboring municipalities (22.0 percent), which provides support for the need to conduct case-based research to offer guidelines, lessons learned, or benchmarks. Compared with the figures regarding practitioners' likelihood of turning to neighboring judicial districts (11.0 percent) and states (8.0 percent), it appears that such benchmarks should emphasize the local level and the context-specific nature of issues relating to eminent domain, a theme that frequently emerged during the interviews. About the same percentage of administrators reported that they were very likely to turn to professional organizations (26.0 percent) and professional conferences (22.0 percent). As evidence of the value of networking among professionals, this also speaks to academics' perhaps making it a higher priority to disseminate research findings via professional conferences.

Finally, the administrators who participated in this research responded that they were about equally likely to turn to academic journal articles (16.0 percent), law review articles (19.0 percent), community organizations (14.0 percent), and interest groups (13.0 percent). Administrators are as likely to turn to the ivory tower as they are to the grassroots, *very interesting*. A town manager aptly described this relationship as "tempering authoritative information in a practical setting."

This soup to nuts examination of where administrators turn for eminent domain guidance provides incredible insights into their use of administrative discretion in the implementation of a legal case, *Kelo*. These findings have resulted in several significant implications for practitioners, scholars, and students of public administration. First, inclusion of the property owner's perspective is a welcome surprise, given the concerns expressed by the literature, and is strongly tied to individual rights' arguments made by administrators who participated in the interviews.

Second, practitioners reported being twice as likely to turn to peers or colleagues in their search for eminent domain guidance as they are to turn to their direct supervisor. They are also equally likely to turn to municipal elected officials as they are to turn to municipal administrators. These findings present significant theoretical implications for the research on hierarchical governance, administrative discretion, and the politics-administration dichotomy. These findings do provide insight into how administrators at different levels interact with one another. Further, this research shows support for the absence, or minimization, at the very least, for the existence of the politics-administration dichotomy at the local government level. Decisions surrounding where an administrator will turn for guidance are a strong invocation of administrative discretion. Practitioners who participated in this study have shown that top-down decision-making occurs less frequently than does bottom-up and that distinctions between career civil servants and elected or appointed officials as sources of guidance are virtually non-existent.

With regard to administrators' being more likely to turn to peers or colleagues than to their direct supervisor during their search for eminent domain guidance, this appears to be due to the level of professional experience of peers and colleagues with relevant issues, compared with direct supervisors. The former have more highly specialized skills, whereas supervisors have broader training and responsibilities. As one planner explained, technical questions would be directed to the planning commission of the municipality because of their targeted expertise in the area. During the interviews, administrators overwhelmingly supported the notion that there is no strict politics-administration dichotomy at the local level. Described as "working hand-in-hand" and "everybody's gotta work with everybody else," administrators who participated in this study reported few boundaries between elected officials and what one town manager called "professional administrators" regarding the blending of duties.

The general sentiment with regard to the relationship between elected officials and administrators at the local level is that it is reciprocal and "service-oriented," according to a planner. As several administrators explained, this relationship is the result of two primary factors. Administrators know that their role is to implement the decisions of the elected officials, but both are comfortable in seeking and providing guidance on specific issues, sometimes whether such guidance is requested or not, as one administrator/elected official explained. Moreover, if elected officials act in an irresponsible manner, or as "a maverick," according to one selectman, they will not be re-elected. Coupled with the low turnover of administrators, even at the department-head level, this gives administrators a "we'll be here long after you're gone" perspective to some extent.[1]

Third, administrators' reliance on professional organizations and conferences during their search for guidance has implications of theoretical and practical import. Theoretically, the literature could benefit from the insight provided by the findings of this study in that administrators view these networking opportunities as about equal to their previous professional experiences. Add to the equation that administrators are more likely to rely on their peers, colleagues, and municipal administrators and elected officials than on their own professional experience. The role of professional experience, networking, and relationship-building in administrators' search for eminent domain guidance, therefore, appears to be quite complex.

Practically, administrators' reliance on professional organizations and conferences provides insight into how academics may work more collaboratively with practitioners. Disseminating information through professional conferences is valued in academia, but it appears to be secondary to the goal of academic publications. The results of this study indicate that perhaps academics should lend consideration to increasing efforts to share the findings of our research with practitioners at conferences. A land use attorney even specifically noted during the interview that a greater academic presence would be welcomed. Moreover, a number of administrators described a strong reliance on the Connecticut Council of Municipalities, as well as several other professional organizations, such as the International Right of Way Association and the American Planning Association, of which one of the interview participants was an early member of the Connecticut chapter. When asked to elaborate on their strong reliance on professional organizations, administrators who participated in the interview explained that the organizations provide much-needed practical guidance on particular situations.

Finally, the question of whether practitioners of public administration actually turn to academia for guidance is answered, at least in the context of eminent domain. While 16.0 percent of administrators responded that they were very likely to turn to academic journal articles in their search for guidance, 58.0 percent responded that it was quite unlikely that they would rely on our published research. As an applied field, public administration should take these findings seriously. Granted, academia has been making headway in this regard, but the administrators in this study have reported that it is not sufficient.

During the interviews, administrators responded that academic journals were most useful, when they provided practical guidance. A frequent theme expressed by administrators during the interviews was how context-specific eminent domain issues are. When asked how academics could do a better job of making our research more relevant to their work, a number of administrators responded that case studies would be particularly helpful. One town manager noted, "case studies bring in the gray areas . . . the politics . . . the intuitive areas" of the process of eminent domain and other complex issues. A councilman/planner described case studies as telling the "human story" and helping administrators "read between the lines." A representative town meeting official stated that the value of academic journals could be heightened if it explored the "individual impact." These findings are consistent with the recent trends in the field of public administration, particularly in light of the recent American Society for Public Administration (ASPA) taskforce on the applied nature of the MPA degree. The taskforce, as well as the most recent Minnowbrook III meeting, both issue strong calls for public administrationists to conduct more in-depth case study research. Even more supportive of for the need to conduct case-study research on eminent domain is the paucity of empirical research on the subject in scholarship in general.

ADMINISTRATORS' DISCRETION AND SEARCH FOR GUIDANCE

In the previous section, the focus was on reviewing where practitioners are likely to turn for guidance on issues relating to eminent domain. Here, however, involves a more in-depth exploration of relationships between practitioners' use of administrative discretion in their decision-making process when faced with takings.

Reviewing the data in Table 7.2 helps to provide a more comprehensive picture of administrators' use of discretion in their search for takings guidance.[2] These survey results also show what factors are contributing to the development of practitioners' guidance process. Once again, this was a very small survey sample that was designed to be exploratory in nature.

There appears to be strong linkages between practitioners' discretion during administrators' search for guidance in the process of eminent domain. These data also provide support between the influence of discretion and professionalism, as described as their familiarity with relevant materials and professional experience with eminent domain; it appears to influence strongly their search for takings guidance.

What is most interesting here is that the strongest relationships exist between the familiarity variable (i.e., how familiar a practitioner reported being with *Kelo*, local ordinances and state statutes affecting eminent domain, and the Takings Clause of the U.S. Constitution) and the corresponding dimension of how likely they reported referring to each for guidance. For example, practitioners reference to state statutes is most strongly related to familiarity with state statutes (44.9 percent), reference to local ordinances and familiar-

Table 7.2. Administrators' Discretion and Search for Eminent Domain Guidance[1]

Administrators' Discretion and Search for Eminent Domain Guidance					
	Familiarity with *Kelo*	Familiarity with Local Ordinance(s)	Familiarity with State Statute(s)	Familiarity with Takings Clause	Professional Experience with Eminent Domain
Refer to *Kelo*	**28.0%*****	27.0%***	24.6%***	22.6%***	29.7%***
Refer to local ordinances		**35.3%*****	29.8%***	22.1%***	39.4%***
Refer to state statutes	28.0%***	34.6%***	**44.9%*****	32.6%***	56.1%***
Refer to Takings Clause		19.9%***	24.7%***	**26.1%*****	21.1%***

1. The statistical measure of association employed is Somers' d. This measure was used because it is an asymmetrical measure of association, as well as a proportionate reduction in error (PRE) statistic, which means that it provides support for a causal relationship, in addition to helping to reduce the error in predicting the value of the dependent variable dimension. Figures shown are for the percentages, which show the strength and direction of the relationship between practitioners' knowledge and experience (columns) and practitioners' understanding (rows). Asterisks are used to indicate the significance levels of the relationships: * significant at 0.1 (10% likely to occur by chance), **significant at 0.05 (5% likely to occur by chance), *** significant at 0.01 (1% likely to occur by chance).

ity to the same is 35.3 percent, reference to *Kelo* and familiarity to the case is 28.0 percent, and, finally, reference to the Takings Clause and familiarity with the Constitutional provision for the takings power is 26.1 percent.[3]

Practitioners' professional eminent domain experience also produces quite strong relationships with administrators' guidance search. Here, the relationship between experience and administrators' reliance on state statutes produces a value of 56.1 percent, followed by 39.4 percent with reference to local ordinances. This is augmented with 29.7 percent for *Kelo*, and 21.1 percent for the Takings Clause. Again, what these percentages show is how likely practitioners' knowledge and professional experience are to influence their search for eminent domain guidance.

How likely administrators are to turn to *Kelo*, local ordinances and state statutes affecting eminent domain, and the Takings Clause for guidance is largely influenced by their familiarity with each. Thus, administrators who are most familiar with these relevant materials are most likely to refer often to them for guidance on issues dealing with eminent domain. Overall, this provides support for strong relationships between administrators' professionalism and discretion in the implementation of eminent domain.

These findings present significant implications for the study of administrators' search for guidance during the process of eminent domain. That practitioners consistently turn to the resources with which they are most familiar provides evidence that they are heavily reliant on quite limited resources. Perhaps this is an issue of bounded rationality and satisficing or path dependence. Administrators "know what they know," and they do not appear to make substantial efforts to seek strong guidance from outside resources. Coupled with the interview findings regarding administrators' familiarity and external contributing factors, it appears that, although practitioners' familiarity is shaped by external factors, their search for guidance and reliance on resources of utility is quite limited to those resources with which they are most familiar.

It appears that practitioners are experiencing what may be best described as a form of *tunnel vision*. But what is the underlying cause of this tunnel vision? As many administrators explained during the interviews, the power of eminent domain generally lacked controversy before *Kelo*. A selectman noted that the public lacked a "general awareness" of eminent domain pre-*Kelo*. An official on the representative town meeting stated that the public is "apathetic unless it affects their life" and that "people don't research anything" unless there is an immediate need. One administrator who has worked in planning since the 1960s stated, "The average citizen didn't know what the city was doing" with regard to using eminent domain for economic and private development pre-*Kelo*. He added, "Politically, it can't happen anymore because of

Kelo." This sentiment was echoed by a retired chief clerk in a judicial district, who added, "At least the *Kelo* case pretty much put an end to that."

Further, practitioners generally agreed that the case just brought a new potential use for the power to the forefront, therefore causing heightened concern among property owners and public administrators alike. A town manager stated that private development was not thought of as an eminent domain use before the case and that it "earned legitimacy" afterward because it "opened [administrators'] eyes" to the prospect but that it has been "blacklisted as a tool." On the other hand, a land use attorney and redevelopment director described eminent domain for economic and private development as "just another tool in self-determination against 'generica.'" According to a deputy chief clerk, practitioners should not be "shortsighted" in thinking that what happened in *Kelo* could not happen in their municipalities, stating, "Sometimes there are powers and forces . . . an extremely wealthy developer that comes in."

Practitioners are now facing new challenges with the use of eminent domain and encountering increased "distrust," according to one planner, and lacking support from the outset. Many interview participants described the value of building preemptive support for projects that could potentially use eminent domain. During the interviews, a number of administrators explained that the key problem with the *Kelo* situation was the city's handling of the eminent domain process. This was largely due to the lack of informing the public where they could become involved in the process. Whether administrators agreed or disagreed with eminent domain generally and for economic or private development more specifically, they overwhelmingly supported what several interview participants referred to as a "transparent" process. This echoes the concerns of the community members involved with *Kelo*.

According to the interview participants, transparency is so crucial to the process of using eminent domain, whether for a more traditional use or for economic or private development, because of the power it assumes in helping to build public support. As one development director noted, municipalities should do what is good for "the neighborhood as a whole." A representative town meeting official asserted that "the deal has to be broadly acceptable" and that the government must have "deference to the neighborhoods." Public involvement in the process should, according to the interview participants, be done in good faith, rather than merely to meet statutory requirements. The practitioner who has been involved in planning since the 1960s explained that municipalities often get new ideas from the public and can and should incorporate them into the development plan. He continued to explain that "vision planning" should be done to show the public "what can be done." Building on this notion is a selectman who noted that any project must be "politically sell-able" and continued to describe the importance of the public's role in the process by asking, "What makes commissions think their ideas are any better than the property owners?" These are serious implications administrators' exercising their discretion in a way that is both responsive *and* responsible.

This leads to one of the most broadly applicable findings of this book, with regard to political v. legal authority. With few exceptions, practitioners who participated in these interviews were overwhelmingly clear that political authority trumps legal authority, as shown in Figure 6.1 of the typology of administrators' discretion. These exceptions relate to administrators' understanding and interpretation of public use, public purpose, public good, and public interest and will be addressed in more detail.

"The town is the people," said one selectman, so the government should agree with the political will of the community. Administrators should try to build support for the project that could potentially require the use of eminent domain, or pre-condemnation negotiation strategies, by "try[ing] to sell the project," according to a landuse chair; "building consensus" before the project moves forward, maintained a planner; or incorporating the "intent of the neighborhood," said another planner.

When asked how the government would handle a situation in which the public was not supportive of the plan, overwhelmingly, practitioners responded that the plan would not progress. Responses offered as to why the plan would be stopped ranged from political fallout, lack of approval for funding, and that residents of the neighborhood "should have more say" than the municipality because they know what is best for their community, according to a development director. The more frequent response, however, surrounded issues associated with political fallout for a decision against the political will of the community.

Practitioners who participated in the interviews expressed a strong understanding that their role was to serve the public and to make decisions aligned with the will of the public, again, responsive *and* responsible. Fear of not being re-elected was certainly a contributing factor for elected officials, but the sentiment generally appeared to be secondary to the notion of public service. The idea of political and legal authority was broadly described by a chairman of the zoning board of appeals as serving as "theoretical checks and balances" on municipal government and service to the public. One selectman noted that he "would go along with his constituents" unless the use of eminent domain was "absolutely necessary," which he equated to issues of public safety, such as road-widening. A representative town meeting official stated that absent public use, which he defined as a "complete use by the public," "individual rights are above the rights of the general public," thus requiring the protection of private property. A selectman echoed this sentiment, noting that it is not "any municipality's business to favor one constituency over another constituency in eminent domain." Another representative town meeting official noted that "if the political will wasn't there," the project would be stopped; he continued to explain that in the representative town meeting style of government, it is "difficult for stupid things to get far" because of the many administrators and opinions involved. The other representative town meeting official countered that this form of government has its downsides because "good ideas don't get through [either] because there are too many opinions."

Though administrators who were interviewed overwhelmingly reported that they would follow the will of the public with regard to political v. legal authority, a handful of administrators advocated a different approach. Reminiscent of the framers of the Constitution, these administrators' perspective on implementing eminent domain against the will of the people was that doing so was the more responsible action. Here, the broader theme, as expressed by this group of administrators, is that some circumstances require administrators to act against the public will for the public interest.

During the interview with the land use attorney and the redevelopment director, they explained that a majority of development projects potentially involving eminent domain, about 80 percent, result in successful pre-condemnation negotiations and strategies. In instances when this is not the result, however, this municipality advocates the use of eminent domain because "it's good for businesses, residents, and the city." In perhaps the most articulate explanation of how a municipality is able to defy the political will of the public in the employment of its eminent domain power, these administrators described the process as "place-making," or "creating a sense of place." These administrators explained that their municipality is faced with the question of "How do you get redevelopment to happen without private funds, absent city funds?" Their response is the creative use of public-private development partnerships.

Public-private development partnerships present the opportunity to advance the public good through economic development and redevelopment while using private, as opposed to municipal, funding. According to the redevelopment director, "It's a great energy to harness, while serving a larger public good." Though the private developer's involvement in the process is self-interest, using those funds creates greater benefits to the community as a whole. These public benefits are not limited to increased tax revenue and job growth, as was the case in *Kelo*. These practitioners described a number of projects that incorporated tangible benefits to the public, such as transit-oriented development projects to bring more residents, visitors, and investments into the city; the moving of existing businesses to premium locations to help their business grow; using partial takings to allow property owners to remain in their current location, while receiving compensation packages based on the redeveloped community; and even something as outside-the-box as moving an auto-repair business to a parking garage located at the center of the transit-oriented development project. As these administrators explained the process, it is significant to involve the public in the process to identify their wants and needs for the community. By incorporating these plans into the overall development plan, the public is more supportive because they were involved in the process and understand how it will benefit their community.

These creative uses of development projects were echoed by the development director of another municipality. Though this administrator responded that she would not continue with a plan that the community did not support, she described the ways in which the development projects seek to incorporate broader public benefits. One example she offered was that instead of building condominiums, the redevelopment plan included duplexes with garages. By offering the same amenities that residents expect in the suburbs, the plan was able to keep existing residents and lure additional people to live and invest in the community.

Though reluctant to make a decision against the public will, one councilman noted that "elected officials shouldn't make decisions in a vacuum." He continued, however: "The public isn't looking at it at the level I am." He proposes a balancing test between serving the public interest and protecting private property, and if that balance were met, he would support a development plan involving eminent domain.

Further, the practitioner involved in planning since the 1960s strongly supported following the public will and stressed the importance of the public's participation in the process. He aptly noted, "It doesn't always matter if the public doesn't agree." Here, his perspective is based off of nearly forty years' experience in planning and having been directly involved in the redevelopment efforts of the 1950s and 60s that are frequently referred to as "negro removal" because of the effects on minority neighborhoods. "Cities burned," he stated, which "led to distrust" in municipal development efforts. But if the proposed plan involves economic or private development and meets with the "intent of the neighborhood" design, he would support the plan.

PUBLIC GOOD, PUBLIC INTEREST, PUBLIC USE, PUBLIC PURPOSE, AND JUST COMPENSATION IN IMPLEMENTING EMINENT DOMAIN

Practitioners who participated in the research for this book were also asked questions about differences between notions of "public good" and "public interest," "public use" and "public purpose," and "just compensation." Much of this relates to how administrators use their discretion in the implementation of policies that are often vague and may use these phrases inter-changeably, in conflict, or in ways that lack substantive meaning. Many administrators noted the difficulties associated with distinguishing between such nuanced phrases as public use, good, purpose, and interest in the context of eminent domain. One land use chair responded that there was no "bright-line test" for knowing the difference. A survey participant responded, "The importance of the definitions is the ways in which they relate to the specifics of the issue," a sentiment echoed by a number of practitioners. The problem, as one administrator aptly explained, is that distinctions are not objective, but they should not be subjective, either. During the interviews, the general response to questions surrounding these phrases was that practitioners acknowledge that there are distinctions. More importantly, however, they are so difficult to make and are largely dependent on the particulars of a given situation, the practitioners do not further investigate the distinctions unless they need to because of an immediate issue.

When asked about "just compensation," however, practitioners generally supported a compensation package that extends beyond the fair-market value of the property being taken. Remember that the Supreme Court has decided that just compensation with eminent domain is limited to the market-value. Noted in open-ended survey responses, such might include relocation assistance or moving expenses, a consideration that the taking is not voluntary, and should be "weighted to the individual property affected." To be sure, practitioners did not advocate what one respondent described as "lavish compensation," but that property owners should be more fully compensated than simply the market value of the property. Practitioners who participated in the interviews echoed these sentiments, describing compensation packages that include many of these considerations, as previously discussed.

Between the survey's open-ended responses and the interviews, several significant findings have emerged with regard to administrators' interpretations of eminent domain policy post-*Kelo*. First, as a land use chair described it, there is a balancing or weighing of two public goods, one of maintaining the public good in preserving an existing community and one of advancing the public good for the broader community. A number of practitioners addressed this balancing test during the interviews, especially in terms of using eminent domain for economic development purposes. As one planner explained, during the 1950s and 60s, eminent domain was used by municipal governments "ostensibly to eliminate urban blight." The result was the destruction of "viable" urban neighborhoods. He continued by stating that previous development projects that emphasized the "bottom-line screwed up the whole redevelopment process."

The problem of using eminent domain in this manner continues today, with some economic development projects clearing out entire neighborhoods "without linking projects to the existing urban fabric," as one survey respondent noted. Rather than rehabilitating existing neighborhoods, municipal plans redevelop entire communities. Practitioners who participated in the interviews addressed the value of preserving communities by involving them in the development process to incorporate their ideas and to maintain the "intent of the neighborhood," both from the perspective of the community members and the municipal government.

This is not limited to distressed or blighted communities, but it also includes historic neighborhoods with a rich cultural history that administrators agreed should be preserved by incorporating it into the development plan. Two examples offered by administrators during the interviews are particularly relevant here. One development director described a recent plan that involved the removal of older, unsuccessful businesses in order to bring a grocery store to the community. Despite the strong presence of private benefit associated with the taking, the community needed and wanted a grocery store and supported the redevelopment plan. In another example, a planner described the process of getting a CVS pharmacy store to locate in the central downtown district. The neighborhood was designed to promote foot traffic, so CVS was required to include parking in the back of the store, a plan that the community supported. Further, the land use attorney and development director stressed the importance of incorporating existing businesses into the development plan; in the municipality's long history of redevelopment and eminent domain, nearly every business affected has relocated to another part of the municipality (with the financial support of the municipality). When businesses are a part of the community and are successful, the community at large benefits from having them remain a part of the community. As a land use chair stated, it is important to "fight for community values" when developing plans and building public support for the project.

Second is the presence of a public need for public use or public purpose in the form of economic development that is based on the particular circumstances of the community. The "need" for a development plan involving the use of eminent domain appears to be related to the circumstances of a community, largely in terms of available land. In more rural municipalities that have land available to develop, practitioners responded that they would be hard-pressed to identify any need to take private property, given the abundance of open land. In more urban municipalities, however, the scarcity of land is more likely to necessitate the use of redevelopment, economic development, and eminent domain. As one survey respondent described the process, "Economic development is critical to a city's survival and the use of eminent domain is critical to older, developed, land-poor cities that need to 'redevelop' rather than build on new virgin lands." Given the varying needs of rural and urban communities, the perspectives of their administrators are largely informed by the circumstances surrounding the municipality's available resources.

Finally, there is the finding regarding the complex nature of practitioners' overwhelming support for an understanding of public use that incorporates some degree of direct public use. Practitioners who participated in the survey broadly supported a definition of public use that allows the public to have direct use of the developed or redeveloped land. What administrators disagree on, however, is what constitutes a public use. Though administrators generally identified roads as being a traditional public use, one first selectman questioned whether there was actually a need for road construction under the public use requirement. In response to those who assert that roads are a public use, she maintained what she described as a more "organic" approach. "Why do roads need to be wider, more direct?" she wondered, continuing that things are more "interesting" when they are not so well-planned. "That's not how things grow well," she concluded. Another administrator, who is a development director, characterized roads as being a public purpose, limiting public uses to schools and possibly parks. With regard to roads and railroads, one representative town meeting official described public use as "complete public use" and continued to assert that both roads and railroads for transportation met the burden of public use.

Most significantly, a number of administrators described ideas of public use and public purpose as being "used more or less interchangeably by us lay people," "all relatively the same," and "one in the same." Moreover, these administrators also discussed the complexity of the phrases when put into practical use, noting that distinctions are more "nuanced" and important in the context of particular situations. One administrator stated, "I very much believe that these need to be better defined within government."

With regard to public good and public interest, public interest appears to have broader implications when employed in a project that could potentially use eminent domain. As one development director noted, "You chose your words based on a project," meaning that distinctions between the phrases are critical during the phase of building public support for a project. Several administrators described public good as being something on a more individual level, whereas public interest signifies larger benefits to the community as a whole. To explain this distinction, one assessor noted, "What might be perceived as the public good might not always be in the public interest." As an example, this practitioner explained how there was a public garden that residents of the municipality, largely residents of apartments, had maintained for about ten years. This garden was located in a public park on the boundary next to the baseball field. The "baseball people" wanted to move the garden to another location in the park to make way for additional parking for the baseball facilities. The "garden people," however, were strongly opposed and quickly mobilized opposition forces. In the end, the garden prevailed. Here, additional parking for the baseball facilities was more in the public good than maintaining the location of the garden, but it was not in the broader public interest, as expressed by the community. According to the assessor, "It's all a numbers game . . . it's the squeaky wheel." Because of the mobilization of the "garden people," the municipality decided not to move the garden.

This example does well to demonstrate distinctions between public good and public interest because it highlights what many practitioners described as the importance of the context of specific situations that could potentially involve the use of eminent domain. Practitioners should be both responsible and responsive to the public will, and reminiscent of the framers' values, sometimes administrators must be more responsible than responsive. This means that some situations require practitioners to act in a manner inconsistent with the public will if those actions will serve a broader public interest. As one selectman aptly noted, "Objectively, people don't always do what's in their interest as a group." Building on the findings regarding legal v. political authority, this presents significant findings in that practitioners who participated in this study are generally more responsive to the public will. Practitioners who described substantial experience with or knowledge of eminent domain explained that, while they would strongly consider the will of the public or lacking public support for a particular project, they would likely support the project if it served a broader public interest. Even one selectman who expressed very strong anti-eminent domain sentiments stated, "You can't be anti-business."

KELO'S INFLUENCE ON PUBLIC V. PRIVATE

For this research, practitioners were asked about their perceptions of the changing character of "public" and "private" post-*Kelo*. Practitioners who responded to open-ended questions generally lacked support for the decision in *Kelo*, though there were many supporters of the Court's ruling in the case. Administrators noted that the case "correctly reaffirmed economic development as a legitimate public interest" and "states have taken a poor and politically expedient route of dealing with this issue." Several practitioners who disagreed with the *Kelo* decision maintained that it "extended eminent domain into areas never used before and certainly not where the framers of the Constitution intended." These practitioners continued to explain that the influence of the case on administrators' understandings of public and private is that it "influenced [the administrator's] belief in the Constitution as written and in [the administrator's] awareness of people attempting to change its original meaning." Other comments included practitioners stating that the case has "made public policy administrators and elected officials think twice before trying to take property by eminent domain" and "following the case and reading the opinions (majority and minority) made a very good exercise." Also important were responses noting that the quasi-public agency, the New London Development Corporation (NLDC), was given far too much power and that the New London project should have incorporated more properties into the project, rather than taking them.

As a number of interview participants explained, one of *Kelo*'s greatest influences on eminent domain and practitioners' understanding is that it "opened their eyes" to a new use of the power. It appears, then, that, while *Kelo* resulted in an increased awareness of using eminent domain for private benefit, practitioners are unlikely to take advantage of this expanded use of the power. During the interviews, practitioners explained *Kelo*'s influence on their understanding of "public" and "private" in the context of eminent domain as being in the form of a heightened awareness. As one selectman stated, "Eminent domain is always going to be there . . . it's not going to meet its death." While eminent domain is not used frequently, as administrators explained in the survey and during the interviews, it is often discussed and is more likely to result in pre-condemnation strategies and negotiations. The changing character of publicness post-*Kelo* appears to be the result of a heightened awareness of the need to guard private property rights from projects involving only an indirect public benefit that is secondary to private gain.

Because administrators described *Kelo*'s influence as opening their eyes to a new use of eminent domain, though it had always been there, their understanding of "public" has been largely shaped by their new understanding of private. As one representative town meeting official described, "Eminent domain shouldn't be considered if the money goes into private pockets." It appears, therefore, that practitioners' understanding of public remains largely unchanged; rather, it is their understanding of the need to provide greater protections for publicness in light of the increased potential for private gain.

In the concluding chapter that follows, significant questions relating to the constitutional and procedural issues of eminent domain and addressed with regard to the findings discussed here. Finally, lessons that may be learned from this in-depth case study of administrative discretion in the context of eminent domain are explored. These are tailored to practitioners of public administration, academics and scholars, and also community members.

NOTES

1. Remember that in the previous chapter on community members' perceptions and understanding, a major concern centered around the inclusion of non-elected, private-sector individuals on the NLDC, the quasi-public organization responsible for managing the *Kelo* takings.

2. Pollock (2005) provides a helpful guide for interpreting the strength of a PRE statistic. For relationships in which the percentage of the statistical measure of association is less than 10 percent, the relationship is weak; relationships between 11 and 20 percent are moderate; relationships between 21 and 30 percent are moderately strong; and relationships greater than 30 percent are strong. He also notes that PRE statistical measures of association indicating a relationship greater than 50 percent are uncommon in social science data, particularly for individual-level survey data.

3. These figures are bolded in Table 7.2 to show the pattern.

Conclusions

For Public Administrators, Public Administrationists, and Community Members

Eminent domain isn't going to meet its death.
—A Connecticut Selectman

In summary, this book is a tool. It is a tool to facilitate transparent, productive dialogue between practitioners and community members on questions and issues relating to eminent domain. Given the discretion that practitioners possess during the takings process, and given the sensationalist coverage of eminent domain, the goal of this book is to educate interested parties about the responsible management of eminent domain. Though this book focuses on the study of eminent domain in light of the recent and controversial *Kelo* decision, its universality rests in its broader emphasis on educating practitioners, community members, scholars, and students.

This book is about the power that administrators wield in the governance process, but it is also about being responsible and responsive to the public good, to the community. By providing a balanced approach that reveals significant findings about practitioners and community members' perspectives on eminent domain, this book begins to uncover comprehensively the content and context of takings and the big-picture of the governance process. Findings of practical and theoretical utility, as well as lessons that may be learned from this study, help to provide a foundational understanding on which to engage in critical reflection, or praxis.

CONSTITUTIONAL QUESTIONS OF PUBLIC USE AND JUST COMPENSATION

Constitutional questions surrounding eminent domain largely encompass two key areas: public use and just compensation. As the only limitations expressed in the Takings Clause of the Constitution, these requirements are at the center of the debate. For issues regarding public use, the main questions are: the broad interpretation of public use as public purpose, as well as the narrow review of the mechanics and purpose of takings. Concerning just compensation, two questions that are the focus include: just compensation as heightened standard in light of the erosion of the public use requirement and exploring alternative compensation models.

These constitutional questions may be thought of as being normative in nature, as they are concerned with the way things *should* be; they involve issues of when and why eminent domain should be used. Concerns that narrow review of takings and the erosion of public use have resulted in insufficient protections for property owners may be somewhat alleviated by the findings of this book. Takings for private development are especially relevant, as *Kelo* has brought these types of takings to light. Practitioners participating in this research overwhelmingly disagree with eminent domain for private development.

Whether or not takings for private development should be made unconstitutional, then, becomes less of a concern, given practitioners' orientations. The focus should shift toward how to educate and inform administrators to understand better the problems associated with such takings. Administrators' overwhelming disdain for private takings warrants some degree of re-direction. Debating the constitutionality of private takings does little to accomplish the true concerns over narrow review and expanding interpretations of public use to include private benefit. With regard for takings for economic development, which has also been a controversial issue, it appears that practitioners consider such takings as encompassing a broader sense of community, compared with the narrow profit-driven nature of private takings. Practitioners do not appear to be taking advantage of the expanded uses of the power of eminent domain post-*Kelo*. Because they overwhelmingly disapprove of eminent domain for private development and strongly support a notion of public use that requires some degree of use by the public, these results provide very strong support for the contention that eminent domain has not "run amok," as many practitioners, property owners, and scholars have feared.

Though the public use requirement may have been eroded by courts and legislatures into a broader public benefit or purpose, those practitioners who actually implement eminent domain proceedings believe there is a need for "use by the public." Given their healthy exercise of administrative discretion, it appears that the Court's expanded interpretations of public use has not opened the eminent domain floodgates quite as wide as has been feared, indicating that *Kelo* has not changed the attitudes of public administrators with regard to using eminent domain more frequently.

Interview participants had particularly valuable insight in this regard. When asked whether eminent domain had always been such a controversial issue, or whether it had heightened post-*Kelo*, results were mixed. A land use chair and a councilman asserted that the public was generally accepting of eminent domain and that *Kelo* had revealed a new use that administrators were unaware they had, thus prompting public outcry. Alternatively, a town manager stated that eminent domain had always been "blacklisted" and a "cultural no-no" as a municipal tool, though acknowledging that *Kelo* "earned legitimacy" for expanded takings. While differences persisted in terms of the disdain for eminent domain before *Kelo*, most administrators who were interviewed described being very cautious about using eminent domain for any reason. Local ordinances or charters are in place that require public hearings "to inform and to educate" the public, as well as mapped-out procedures for takings when the funding is the result of state or federal grants. For the administrators who participated in this research, eminent domain is a last resort, which requires a "justification that no alternative exists," and involves a balancing of governmental needs and the rights of property owners and the community.

Expansive notions of public use as public purpose lead to questions about just compensation being the last remaining protection for property owners, as well as the use of alternative compensation models. Here, practitioners frequently discussed the use of pre-condemnation strategies and negotiations. These administrators generally described using eminent domain as a last resort, and negotiations with property owners assume a major role in the process of implementing eminent domain. As several practitioners explained, once eminent domain proceedings are initiated, the government's hands are tied, and they must pay the property owner just compensation, or fair market value. When property owners engage in negotiations, however, the government will often pay above the market value for the property, in addition to providing relocation assistance and additional forms of compensation. This, then, involves balancing what *should* be paid to the property owners with how much of that cost *should* be transferred to taxpayers.

PROCEDURAL QUESTIONS OF TRANSACTION COSTS AND OVERSIGHT

Procedural questions involving takings emphasize two areas: transaction costs and governmental oversight and accountability. Transaction costs' questions include: inefficiency of these costs and the balancing of governmental goals. With regard to oversight, the two questions are: deference to practitioners and the presence of governmental oversight and flexibility during the implementation process.

While the constitutional questions are normative and focus on the way things *should* be, these procedural questions are quite the opposite. Procedural questions, by their very nature, are more fact-based, they are positive and are concerned with the way things *are*. Procedurally, takings questions in this regard emphasize how eminent domain is implemented. Here, major concerns include the appropriate degree of governmental flexibility in using eminent domain, as well as issues of transparency and accountability. A general theme throughout this research is that the state of Connecticut had substantial takings protections in place during the time of *Kelo*; problems arose, however, because the execution lacked good faith efforts.

Important here is the balancing of costs and benefits of the taking. Much of this sense was strongly tied to the transparency of the takings process. During the interviews, a number of practitioners described the value and significance of building support within the community for a project that could potentially involve the use of eminent domain *before* the issue of eminent domain was even put on the table. What this research finds is that governments generally use takings as a last resort. Practitioners appear to understand the severity of using the power, or *right*, as one administrator called it, of eminent domain. Administrators reported that decisions are not made without serious consideration of the need for the particular project and the projects likely to be taken.

Balancing governmental goals, and the related inefficiency of transaction costs, is also at the forefront of the takings debate. The argument asserts that property owners should be paid above just compensation, market value, and that avoiding the use of eminent domain, in favor of pre-condemnation strategies, minimizes the transaction costs passed on to the public. Practitioners generally indicated that using takings should be avoided where possible, with a number of administrators describing situations involving "unreasonable" property owners as the cause for eminent domain. This fits with issues involving holdouts slowing the process, therefore passing along greater costs to taxpayers. Holdouts, however, are unable to stop the process once eminent domain proceedings are initiated because of statutory restrictions and the rule of law.

Prior to initiating eminent domain proceedings, practitioners advocate the use of negotiations between municipal attorneys, external real estate firms, and elected officials and the property owners. Properties required for the project are assessed, and compensation is determined. The government then balances the costs and benefits of the taking, as well as whether or not the public wants to pay for the property. The decision to initiate eminent domain proceedings involves the balancing of the governmental goals to advance the public good, or to "shape itself in the public interest," as one redevelopment administrator aptly noted, while maintaining the "fabric" of the existing community, in the words of a planner.

Particularly relevant is practitioners' understanding of the idea of just compensation as being *just* to both the property owner and the public having to pay for it. This fits well with the balancing of government goals and previous findings about the public being willing to pay for the compensation package. Practitioners generally understood just compensation as being primarily a legal requirement dictated by statutes, ordinances, and the courts. Therefore, once eminent domain proceedings were initiated, administrators' hands are tied with regard to the amount of compensation they may offer, as it is limited to market value. From the perspective of passing along transaction costs to the public from initiating eminent domain proceedings, the issue is really more about balancing goals than it is about transaction costs. To be sure, eminent domain proceedings are costly, but practitioners expressed greater concern over justly compensating property owners for the taking and their loss. The emphasis is on "paying for goodwill," as one administrator described it, rather than market value.

Moreover, procedural questions surround whether the judiciary or legislature is best-suited to provide oversight, as well as to what degree to allow for governmental flexibility. Practitioners who participated in this research reported a strong reliance on both the judicial and legislative branches during their search for takings guidance. It appears to matter more that practitioners *are* seeking out both of these sources for guidance, rather than which body of government is providing the oversight.

Regarding their use of administrative discretion, practitioners generally exercised a strong dose of prerogative. The idea of establishing some sort of formal review is less important in a post-*Kelo* environment filled with heightened discretion and informal authority. Practitioners reported being most likely to turn to peers and colleagues and professional networks for guidance, rather than traditional hierarchical governance structures. What this shows is that it is more important to focus on better informing the resources to which practitioners turn, instead of emphasizing and debating the establishment of some formal standard of review. Most important, however, is that practitioners reported a strong reliance on local ordinances and state statutes affecting eminent domain. This shows that the focus should shift toward educating and better developing resources that they were less likely to turn for guidance, such as professional conferences and organizations, for future guidance.

LESSONS LEARNED FOR PUBLIC ADMINISTRATORS

Because practitioners who must implement eminent domain are afforded (and are exercising) a great deal of deference in initiating such proceedings, it is important that their understanding of relevant issues includes multiple perspectives and considerations. When necessitated by a particular situation, these administrators seek guidance on eminent domain from professionally appropriate resources, such as local ordinances and state statutes affecting eminent domain, state and federal Constitutions and Supreme Court decisions, and a strong consideration for the perspective of property owners.

Concern remains, however, that administrators are only marginally seeking out further understanding and guidance when an issue related to eminent domain presents an immediate need, thus the tunnel vision they appear to be experiencing. Strong reliance on limited resources, albeit professional foci supported by the literature, prohibits administrators from taking full advantage of the resources at their disposal. As evidenced by the typology on administrators' understanding, there is a general sense that eminent domain should be avoided at all costs by seeking alternative development plans and pre-condemnation negotiations and strategies. But, as one selectman aptly noted, "Eminent domain isn't going to meet its death."

Practitioners should exercise their discretion in a manner involving an active, rather than passive, role in the implementation process based on expertise, competence, and good-faith efforts. Given all of this, administrators would be well-advised to consider broadening the scope of their search for eminent domain guidance. Doing so may result in an enhanced understanding of issues related to eminent domain. Such might be broadly described as deeper insight into the balance between responsibility and responsiveness.

The erosion of the public use requirement and narrow role of review of takings do not appear to be such grave concerns as the relevant eminent domain research suggests. Practitioners support narrow interpretations of public use and generally do not require strong review by the judiciary or legislatures to keep their use of the power, or right, of eminent domain in check because they turn to these resources for guidance absent any formal requirement. Moreover, practitioners take seriously the just compensation requirement and frequently reported using alternative compensation models to pay appropriately property owners involved in takings. Related is administrators' use of pre-condemnation strategies to achieve a compensation that is just to both property owners and the public who must pay the compensation.

But is being responsible enough to ensure that administrators are fulfilling their role to serve the public interest? What role should responsiveness assume in the process? How might the two be balanced? The typology of administrators' understanding (i.e., place-makers, responders, opportunists, and content administrators) shows practitioners' attempts at balancing being responsible and responsive. Few practitioners, namely the place-makers, expressed an ability, or willingness, to forgo responsiveness in the interest of being responsible. This speaks to the difficulties associated with the political v. legal authority of eminent domain and administrators' use of discretion and professionalism when faced with circumstances involving implementation in this context. In other words, this typology offers insight into the balance that practitioners attempt to strike between improving the community via eminent domain, or being responsible, and responding to the public will, or responsiveness. The contributions of the typology also address broader issues of the use of administrative discretion in making decisions surrounding this balancing act.

These findings suggest that practitioners generally do balance the needs of the government, the property owners, and the public; it is a balancing of multiple public goods. As one administrator described it during our interview, eminent domain is a useful tool for communities to employ when "shaping themselves in the public interest." This notion truly speaks to what is simultaneously a power and a duty of administrators with regard to eminent domain. What is most important to take away from the findings of this research is that practitioners do genuinely take seriously their role in public service, whether as a professional administrator or an elected official, both generally speaking and specifically in the context of eminent domain.

LESSONS LEARNED FOR PUBLIC ADMINISTRATIONISTS

What this book should convey to scholars of public administration is a sense of direction in the continuing development of empirical and theoretical research on the study of eminent domain. Much of the work on takings is more sensationalist than these findings reveal to be necessary. These interviews with practitioners actually involved in the implementation of eminent domain have highlighted fertile ground for the academic study of takings.

The most obvious lesson learned, of course, is that more empirical case studies of eminent domain should be conducted. Given the inherently context-specific nature of takings, scholars of the field should investigate that deeper level of understanding. Such critical reflection and analysis is incredibly important in developing guidance and resources for practitioners. Administrators frequently described the need for this type of research. Because *Kelo* has changed the way practitioners *do* eminent domain, scholars must change the way research is done to provide more critical analysis of the use and process of eminent domain.

Further, these findings suggest that the focus of research should shift to being a more accurate reflection of what is happening on the ground with front-line practitioners. Rather than engaging in high-minded debates about oversight or constitutionality, public administrationists should actively participate in research that meets the needs of practitioners based on what is actually happening. This is the start of a new era of the field, with regard to eminent domain in a post-*Kelo* environment, and scholars should conduct research that reflects that.

Most importantly, however, academics (and practitioners) should be mindful of the human side of eminent domain. Practitioners who participated in this research expressed a strong understanding of what is at stake when eminent domain is used. Researchers should be cautious about contributing to the sensationalization of takings, as this study has shown such to be inaccurate.

LESSONS LEARNED FOR COMMUNITY MEMBERS

Kelo has brought forth fertile ground for concern among community members about governmental abuses of eminent domain. At the same time, however, it has presented the public with the opportunity to become better informed about issues surrounding takings. There is a fine distinction between law and policy, and *Kelo* has highlighted (and then blurred) that line. As a matter of law, the case followed state statutes and constitutional precedents. As a matter of policy, a nation-wide debate continues to evolve.

Hopefully, this book can serve as a resource for community members involved with eminent domain. There are a number of valuable resources to which grassroots organizers can turn to become more responsible in developing an understanding of relevant issues. Moreover, this study shows the resources that the government uses for guidance, so community members would be well-advised to seek out these publically-available resources, as well.

What that means is to be aware of which local ordinances and state statutes are relevant and to become familiar with them. Becoming involved in the discussions about governmental projects that may involve the use of eminent domain translates into becoming educated and asking questions of governmental officials. Just as practitioners should actively seek to involve and educate the public about these issues, community members should hold themselves responsible for asking questions and seeking active representation at the table.

Appendix A: Demographic Characteristics of Study Participants

DEMOGRAPHIC CHARACTERISTICS OF STUDY PARTICIPANTS		
Variable	Frequency	Percent
Level of government		
Municipality	135	95.1
Judicial District	3	2.1
Other	4	2.8
Gained employment		
Appointed	51	35.9
Career civil servant	28	19.7
Elected	53	37.3
Other	10	7.0
Employment status		
Full-time	103	72.5
Part-time	36	25.4
Department employed		
Assessor	23	16.2
Attorney	4	2.8
Building	4	2.8
Economic development	4	2.8
Manager	12	8.5
Mayor	5	3.5
Planning	12	8.5
Representative town meeting	9	6.3
Town clerk	12	8.5
Town council	14	9.9

Variable	Frequency	Percent
Zoning	3	2.1
Board of aldermen	3	2.1
Board of assessment appeals	0	0.0
Board of ethics	0	0.0
Board of selectmen	16	11.3
Housing authority	0	0.0
Planning commission	0	0.0
Zoning board of appeals	1	0.7
Judicial district clerk's office	3	2.1
Other	10	7.0
Landuse	5	3.5
Redevelopment[1]	2	1.4
Employment responsibilities		
Administrative	94	66.0
Budgeting or financial management	82	58.0
Community outreach	56	39.0
Conduct research	39	27.0
Contracts	48	34.0
Department head	63	44.0
Develop programs	38	27.0
Economic development	45	32.0
Evaluate programs	41	29.0
Grants	46	32.0
Human resources	28	20.0
Implement programs	49	35.0
Legal	28	20.0
Legislative work	47	33.0
Lobby	20	14.0
Manage programs	52	37.0
Planning	54	38.0
Policy or program analyst	27	19.0
Supervisory responsibilities	72	51.0
Other	23	16.0
Tenure living in CT		
Less than 6 months	1	0.7
6 months to 1 year	0	0.0
2 to 3 years	0	0.0
4 to 5 years	1	0.7
6 to 10 years	6	4.2
More than 10 years	134	94.4

Variable	Frequency	Percent
Tenure holding current position		
Less than 6 months	2	1.4
6 months to 1 year	9	6.3
2 to 3 years	32	22.5
4 to 5 years	25	17.6
6 to 10 years	28	19.7
More than 10 years	46	32.4
Tenure government employment		
Less than 6 months	1	0.7
6 months to 1 year	2	1.4
2 to 3 years	8	5.6
4 to 5 years	13	9.2
6 to 10 years	23	16.2
More than 10 years	83	58.5
Education attained		
HS diploma/equivalency	11	7.7
Associate's degree	20	14.1
Bachelor's degree	42	29.6
Master's degree	48	33.8
Doctoral degree	20	14.1
Currently degree-seeking		
HS diploma/equivalency	1	0.7
Associate's degree	3	2.1
Bachelor's degree	6	4.2
Master's degree	5	3.5
Doctoral degree	2	1.4
Non-degree coursework		
Associate's degree	4	2.8
Bachelor's degree	3	2.1
Master's degree	6	4.2
Doctoral degree	4	2.8
Public service motivation		
Welfare of community	85	60.0
Civic duty of public service	65	46.0
Serve the public interest	102	72.0
Financial security	31	22.0
Champion public causes	44	31.0
Program/policy formation process	65	46.0
Other	18	13.0
Gender		
Male	79	56.0
Female	52	37.0

Variable	Frequency	Percent
Age		
18 to 24	1	1.0
25 to 34	11	8.0
35 to 44	22	1.05
45 to 54	45	32.0
55 to 64	36	25.0
65 and above	16	11.0
Ethnicity		
White	119	83.8
Black	2	1.4
Hispanic	3	2.1
Asian	0	0.0
Other	1	0.7

1. The categories of "landuse" and "redevelopment" were not given as response options on the survey but were added during the data cleaning stage as a result of respondents' identification in the "other" option.

Appendix B: Expanded Search for Eminent Domain Guidance

Expanded Search for Eminent Domain Guidance					
Variable	Percent Very Likely[1]	Percent Very Unlikely	Median	Mode	Mean
State ED statute(s)	69	7	6	6	4.96
Local ED ordinance(s)	54	20	5	6	4.30
State Supreme Court decisions	49	18	5	6	4.22
Property owner's perspective	42	22	4	6	3.97
State Constitution	38	29	4	6	3.79
US Supreme Court decisions	36	29	4	6	3.73
Peers or colleagues	32	26	3	3	3.60
Municipal administrator	31	33	3	6	3.48
Municipal elected official	30	34	3	6	3.42
US Constitution	30	36	3	1	3.40
Professional experience	26	48	2	1	2.90
Professional organizations	26	32	3	1	3.24
State elected official	24	39	3	1	3.18
Professional conferences	22	40	3	1	2.98
Neighboring municipalities	22	27	3	3	3.31
Law review articles	19	47	3	1	2.80
State administrator	16	48	2	1	2.71
Academic journal articles	16	58	2	1	2.51

Variable	Percent Very Likely[1]	Percent Very Unlikely	Median	Mode	Mean
Direct supervisor	15	62	1	1	2.22
JD administrator	14	61	2	1	2.29
Community organizations	14	46	2	1	2.70
Interest groups	13	54	2	1	2.48
Neighboring JDs	11	51	2	1	2.44
Colleges or universities	11	63	2	1	2.23
Personal experience	10	74	1	1	1.87
Family or friends	10	66	2	1	2.13
Local newspapers	9	58	2	1	2.33
Local media	9	66	2	1	2.13
Neighboring states	8	62	2	1	2.15
National newspapers	7	65	1	1	2.05
National media	4	73	1	1	1.82

1. These percentages are based on the total number of survey responses for each question. The left column includes response options of 5 to 6 to show the highest likelihood; the right column includes response options of 1 to 2 to show the lowest likelihood.

Appendix C: Survey Instrument

1. Which level of government best describes your current employment?
    a. Municipality
    b. Judicial district
    c. Other

2. Which best describes the way in which you gained your current employment?
    a. Appointed
    b. Career civil servant
    c. Elected
    d. Other

3. Are you employed full-time or part-time?
    a. Full-time
    b. Part-time

4. In which department are you currently employed?
    a. Assessor
    b. Attorney
    c. Building
    d. Economic development
    e. Manager
    f. Mayor
    g. Planning
    h. Representative town meeting

i. Town clerk
j. Town council
k. Zoning
l. Board of alderman
m. Board of assessment appeals
n. Board of ethics
o. Board of selectmen
p. Housing authority
q. Planning commission
r. Zoning board of appeals
s. Judicial district clerk's office
t. Other

5. Which of the following below describe your responsibilities in your current employment? *Check all that apply.*

a. Administrative ______
b. Budgeting or financial management ______
c. Community outreach ______
d. Conduct research ______
e. Contracts ______
f. Department head ______
g. Develop programs ______
h. Economic development ______
i. Evaluate programs ______
j Grants ______
k. Human resources ______
l. Implement programs ______
m. Legal ______
n. Legislative work ______
o. Lobby ______
p. Manage programs ______
q. Planning ______
r. Policy or program analyst ______
s. Supervisory responsibilities ______
t. Other *(list as many as necessary):* ______

6. How long have you:

a. Lived in Connecticut:

< 6 months	6 months–1 year	2–3 years	4–5 years	6–10 years	> 10 Years

b. Held your current position:

< 6 months	6 months–1 year	2–3 years	4–5 years	6–10 years	> 10 Years

c. Been employed by the government in any capacity:

< 6 months	6 months–1 year	2–3 years	4–5 years	6–10 years	> 10 Years

7. How would you describe your educational background in each of the following below?

   a. Highest level of education you have attained:

HS diploma/ equiv.	Associate's	Bachelor's	Master's	Doctoral

   b. Currently working on any degree:

HS diploma/ equiv.	Associate's	Bachelor's	Master's	Doctoral

   c. Completed non-degree-seeking coursework at the level of:

Associate's	Bachelor's	Master's	Doctoral

8. If you hold, are currently working on, or have completed non-degree-seeking coursework in a master's or doctoral degree, please list your field of study for each.

   a. Master's:
   b. Doctoral:

9. If you have participated in any formal professional training related to eminent domain for your current position, please describe.

10. Please describe what motivated you for a career in public service. *Check all that apply.*

    a. Concern for the welfare of the community ______
    b. Consider public service a civic duty ______
    c. Desire to service the public interest ______
    d. Financial security ______
    e. Opportunity to champion public causes ______
    f. Participation in the process of program or policy formation ______
    g. Other *(list as many as necessary)*: ______

11. How familiar are you with each of the following below? *Please respond on a scale of 1 to 6 (1=not at all; 6=very familiar).*

	Not at all					*Very familiar*
a. US Supreme Court's ruling in *Kelo v. City of New London*:	1	2	3	4	5	6
b. Local ordinance(s) affecting eminent domain:	1	2	3	4	5	6
c. State statutes(s) affecting eminent domain:	1	2	3	4	5	6
d. Takings Clause of the 5th Amendment of the US Constitution:	1	2	3	4	5	6

12. How many times have you read each of the following below?

a. *Kelo* case:
Never   Once   2 to 3   4 to 5   More than 5

b. Local ordinance(s) affecting eminent domain:
Never   Once   2 to 3   4 to 5   More than 5

c. State statutes(s) affecting eminent domain:
Never   Once   2 to 3   4 to 5   More than 5

d. Takings Clause of the 5th Amendment of the US Constitution:
Never   Once   2 to 3   4 to 5   More than 5

13. Were you required to read each of the following below as part of your job responsibilities?

a. *Kelo* case:	Yes	No
b. Local ordinance(s) affecting eminent domain:	Yes	No
c. State statutes(s) affecting eminent domain:	Yes	No
d. Takings Clause of the 5th Amendment of the US Constitution:	Yes	No

14. How often do you refer to each of the following below for clarification or information when dealing with an issue related to eminent domain? *Please respond on a scale of 1 to 6 (1=not at all; 6=very often).*

	Not at all					*Very often*
a. *Kelo* case:	1	2	3	4	5	6
b. Local ordinance(s) affecting eminent domain:	1	2	3	4	5	6
c. State statute(s) affecting eminent domain:	1	2	3	4	5	6
d. Takings Clause of the 5th Amendment of the US Constitution:	1	2	3	4	5	6

15. How closely did you follow the *Kelo* case in each of the following below? *Please respond on a scale of 1 to 6 (1=not at all; 6=very closely).*

	Not at all					*Very closely*
a. Local newspapers:	1	2	3	4	5	6
b. National newspapers:	1	2	3	4	5	6
c. Local media (excluding newspapers):	1	2	3	4	5	6
d. National media (excluding newspapers):	1	2	3	4	5	6

16. How familiar are you with the precedent cases discussed in the *Kelo* case? *Please respond on a scale of 1 to 6 (1=not at all; 6=very familiar).*

Not at all					*Very familiar*
1	2	3	4	5	6

17. How applicable do you think the Takings Clause of the 5th Amendment of the US Constitution is to eminent domain in your municipality or judicial district? *Please respond on a scale of 1 to 6 (1=not at all; 6=very applicable).*

Not at all					*Very applicable*
1	2	3	4	5	6

18. How frequently have you been involved with eminent domain in each of the following below? *Please respond on a scale of 1 to 6 (1=not at all; 6=very frequently).*

	Not at all					*Very frequently*
a. Professionally:	1	2	3	4	5	6
b. Personally:	1	2	3	4	5	6

19. How frequently does your municipality or judicial district contract with private firms on issues related to eminent domain? *Please respond on a scale of 1 to 6 (1=not at all; 6=very frequently).*

Not at all					*Very frequently*	*Don't know*
1	2	3	4	5	6	7

20. It would be very helpful if you could please describe the conditions under which your municipality or judicial district would likely contract with private firms on issues related to eminent domain (if applicable). *This information would be very helpful, but you may leave it blank if you wish.*

21. In general, how significantly has the *Kelo* case impacted the use of eminent domain in your municipality or judicial district? *Please respond on a scale of 1 to 6 (1=not at all; 6=very significantly).*

Not at all					*Very significantly*	*Don't know*
1	2	3	4	5	6	7

22. Based on your perception, in general, how significantly has the *Kelo* case impacted each of the following below in your municipality or judicial district? *Please respond on a scale of 1 to 6 (1=not at all; 6=very significantly).*

	Not at all					*Very significantly*	*Don't know*
a. Number of takings:	1	2	3	4	5	6	7
b. Use of pre-condemnation strategies:	1	2	3	4	5	6	7
c. Contracting with private firms:	1	2	3	4	5	6	7
d. Amount of consideration you afford the local media:	1	2	3	4	5	6	7
e. Amount of consideration you afford the national media:	1	2	3	4	5	6	7

23. Based on your perception, in general, how have each of the following below changed in your municipality or judicial district since the *Kelo* case?

   a. Number of takings:

   No noticeable change Decreased Increased Don't know

   b. Use of pre-condemnation strategies:

   No noticeable change Decreased Increased Don't know

   c. Contracting with private firms:

   No noticeable change Decreased Increased Don't know

   d. Amount of consideration you afford the local media:

   No noticeable change Decreased Increased Don't know

e. Amount of consideration you afford the national media:
No noticeable change Decreased Increased Don't know

24. It would be very helpful if you could please describe any pre-condemnation strategies that your municipality or judicial district uses more frequently since the *Kelo* case (if applicable). *This information would be very helpful, but you may leave it blank if you wish.*

25. How strongly do you agree with each of the following below? *Please respond on a scale of 1 to 6 (1=not at all; 6=strongly agree).*

	Not at all					*Strongly agree*
a. Use of eminent domain in general:	1	2	3	4	5	6
b. *Kelo* case:	1	2	3	4	5	6
c. Use of eminent domain for private development:	1	2	3	4	5	6
d. Use of eminent domain for economic development:	1	2	3	4	5	6

26. How well do you understand each of the following below? *Please respond on a scale of 1 to 6 (1=not at all; 6= very well).*

	Not at all					*Very well*
a. Eminent domain:	1	2	3	4	5	6
b. *Kelo* case:	1	2	3	4	5	6

27. The following is a very detailed question, and I appreciate your efforts at answering it as thoroughly as possible. When you are in need of guidance on an issue related to eminent domain, how likely are you to turn to each of the following below for guidance? *Please respond on a scale of 1 to 6 (1=not at all; 6=very likely for each item a through ff).*

	Not at all					*Very likely*
a. Academic journal articles (excluding law review articles):	1	2	3	4	5	6
b. Law review articles:	1	2	3	4	5	6
c. Local eminent domain ordinance(s):	1	2	3	4	5	6
d. State eminent domain statutes(s):	1	2	3	4	5	6
e. US Constitution:	1	2	3	4	5	6

f.	US Supreme Court decisions:	1	2	3	4	5	6
g.	State Constitution:	1	2	3	4	5	6
h.	State court decisions:	1	2	3	4	5	6
i.	Your previous professional experience:	1	2	3	4	5	6
j.	Your previous personal experience:	1	2	3	4	5	6
k.	Your direct supervisor:	1	2	3	4	5	6
l.	Your peers or colleagues:	1	2	3	4	5	6
m.	Administrator in your municipality:	1	2	3	4	5	6
n.	Administrator in your judicial district:	1	2	3	4	5	6
o.	Administrator in your state:	1	2	3	4	5	6
p.	Elected official in your municipality:	1	2	3	4	5	6
q.	Elected official in your state:	1	2	3	4	5	6
r.	Property owner's perspective:	1	2	3	4	5	6
s.	Family or friends:	1	2	3	4	5	6
t.	Community organizations:	1	2	3	4	5	6
u.	Interest groups:	1	2	3	4	5	6
v.	Professional conferences:	1	2	3	4	5	6
w.	Professional organizations:	1	2	3	4	5	6
x.	Local newspapers:	1	2	3	4	5	6
y.	National newspapers:	1	2	3	4	5	6
z.	Local media (excluding newspapers):	1	2	3	4	5	6
aa.	National media (excluding newspapers):	1	2	3	4	5	6
bb.	Neighboring municipalities:	1	2	3	4	5	6
cc.	Neighboring judicial districts:	1	2	3	4	5	6
dd.	Neighboring states:	1	2	3	4	5	6
ee.	Colleges or universities:	1	2	3	4	5	6
ff.	Other (*list as many as necessary*):	1	2	3	4	5	6

28. Do you have any comments about your answers in Question 27 above? *This information would be very helpful, but you may leave it blank if you wish.*

29. How well does each of the following general definitions below adequately cover your experiences surrounding the terms? *Please respond on a scale of 1 to 6 (1=not at all; 6=very well).*

		Not at all					*Very well*
a.	"Public use" is generally described as "Use by the public involving a right on the part of the public, or some portion of it, or some public or quasi-public agency on behalf of the public":	1	2	3	4	5	6

b. "Public purpose" is generally described as "A use of public property for any purpose must be an exclusive use by the public, open to all the people on a basis of equality to such extent as the capacity of the property admits, or an exclusive use by some public or quasi-public agency on behalf of the public": 1 2 3 4 5 6
c. "Public good" is generally described as "A variety of interests . . . the primary social interests of safety, order, and morals": 1 2 3 4 5 6
d. "Public interest" is generally described as "Matters of general right or interest . . . more than an interest on the part of many members of the public from the standpoint of an individual": 1 2 3 4 5 6
e. "Just compensation" is generally described as "A compensation which is just, not merely to the individual whose property is taken, but to the public which is to pay for it": 1 2 3 4 5 6
f. "Blight" is generally described as "Deterioration of an area or building usually because of lack of maintenance or because of the presence of some external factor causing property values to decline": 1 2 3 4 5 6

30. Do you have any comments about your answers in Question 29 above? *This information would be very helpful, but you may leave it blank if you wish.*

31. When you consider requirements for the use of eminent domain, which of the following are most important? *Please respond by RANKING each of the following below on a scale of 1 to 6 (1=least important; 6=most important). Please assign each number to only one choice below.*

a. Public use
b. Public purpose
c. Public good
d. Public interest
e. Just compensation
f. Blight

32. Do you have any comments about your answers in Question 31 above? *This information would be very helpful, but you may leave it blank if you wish.*

33. How strongly do you agree with each of the following below? *Please respond on a scale of 1 to 6 (1=not at all; 6=strongly agree).*

	Not at all					*Strongly agree*
a. "Public use" is most similar to "public good," and "public purpose" is most similar to "public interest":	1	2	3	4	5	6
b. "Public use" is most similar to "public interest," and "public purpose" is most similar to "public good":	1	2	3	4	5	6

34. Do you have any comments about your answers in Question 33 above? *This information would be very helpful, but you may leave it blank if you wish.*

35. How significantly has the *Kelo* case influenced each of the following below? *Please respond on a scale of 1 to 6 (1=not at all; 6=very significantly).*

	Not at all					*Very significantly*
a. Your understanding of "public" in the context of eminent domain:	1	2	3	4	5	6
b. Your understanding of "private" in the context of eminent domain:	1	2	3	4	5	6

36. Do you have any comments about your answers in Question 35 above? *This information would be very helpful, but you may leave it blank if you wish.*

This information would be helpful, but you may leave it blank if you wish.

37. Please state the name of the municipality or judicial district in which you are currently employed.

38. What is your gender? Male Female

39. What is your age? 18–24 25–34 35–44 45–54 55–64 65 and above

40. With what ethnic background do you identify? White Black Hispanic Asian Other:

41. OPTIONAL INTERVIEW REQUEST QUESTION: If you are interested in participating in an interview with me, please include the following contact information. By completing this interview request question, you are agreeing that you have read the above information about my study and are consenting to participate in the interview part of the study.
    a. Name:
    b. Title:
    c. Municipality or judicial district:
    d. Email address:
    e. Phone number:

References

Bamberger, K. A. (2008). Normative canons in the review of administrative policy-making. *The Yale Law Journal, 118*, 64–125.

Behn, R. D. (1995). The big questions of public management. *Public Administration Review, 55*, 313–324.

———. (1998). What right do public managers have to lead? *Public Administration Review, 58*, 209–224.

Bell, A. & Parchomovsky, G. (2007). Taking compensation private. *Stanford Law Review, 59*, 871–906.

Benedict, J. (2009). *Little pink house: A true story of defiance and courage.* New York, NY: Grand Central Publishing.

Benson, B. L. (2005). The mythology of holdout as justification for eminent domain and provision of roads. *The Independent Review, 10*, 165–194.

Berman et al., Executors v. Parker et al., 348 U.S. 26 (1954).

Boudreaux, P. (2005). Eminent domain, property rights, and the solution of representative.

Calfee, C. (2006). *Kelo v. City of New London*: The more things stay the same, the more they change. *Ecology Law Quarterly, 33*, 545–581.

Chandler, R. C. (1983). The problem of moral reasoning in American public administration: The case for a code of ethics. *Public Administration Review, 42*, 32–39.

Christensen, T. (2005). From direct "public use" to indirect "public benefit": *Kelo v. New London's* bridge from rational basis to heightened scrutiny from eminent domain takings. *Brigham Young University Law Review, 6*, 1669–1714.

City agencies back NLDC, conditionally. (2000, January 15). *The Day*. Retrieved March 10, 2011, from www.theday.com

Clauretie, T. M., Kuhn, W., & Schwer, R. K. (2004). Residential properties taken under eminent domain: Do government appraisers track market value? *The Journal of Real Estate Research*, 26, 317–327.

Cohen, C. E. (2006). Eminent domain after *Kelo v. City of New London*: An argument for banning economic development takings. *Harvard Journal of Law & Public Policy, 29*, 491–568.

Cook, B. J. (1992). Subordination or independence for administrators? The decision of 1789 reexamined. *Public Administration Review, 52*, 497–503.

———. (1998). Politics, political leadership, and public management. *Public Administration Review, 58*, 225–230.

Councilors say they agonized over Fort Trumbull vote. (2000, January 20). *The Day*. Retrieved March 10, 2011, from www.theday.com.

Cresswell, J. W. & Vicki L. Plano Clark. 2011. *Designing and Conducting Mixed Methods Research*. (2nd ed.) Thousand Oaks, CA: Sage Publications, Inc.

Cypher, M. L. & Forgey, F. A. (2003). Eminent domain: An evaluation based on criteria relating to equity, effectiveness, and efficiency. *Urban Affairs Review, 39*, 254–268.

Denhardt, R. B. (2011). *Theories of public organization* (6th ed.). Boston, MA: Wadsworth, Cengage Learning.

Douglass, B. (1980). The common good and the public interest. *Political Theory, 8*, 103–117.

Dworkin, R. M. (1967). The model of rules. *The University of Chicago Law Review, 35*, 14–46.

Durham, J. G. (1985). Efficient just compensation as a limit on eminent domain. *Minnesota Law Review, 69*, 1277–1313.

Krislov, S. (1974). *Representative bureaucracy*. Englewood Cliffs, NJ: Prentice-Hall, Inc.

Eminent domain: Public hearing before the Planning and Development Committee, Joint Committee, Connecticut (2005) (testimony of Lloyd Beachy).

Enacted legislation since *Kelo*. (2009). Arlington, VA: Castle Coalition. Retrieved April 12, 2010, http://www.castlecoalition.org/index.php?option=com_content&task= view&id=510&Itemid=107.

Esposto, F. G. (1996). The political economy of taking and just compensation. *Public Choice, 89*, 267–282.

Eubanks, E. E. (2004). School desegregation under *Brown*: The role of court master, guidelines and experiences. *The Journal of Negro Education, 73*, 209–217.

Fallbrook Irrigation District v. Bradley, 164 U.S. 112 (1896).

Farjad, N. (2007). Condemnation friendly or land use wise? A broad interpretation of the public use requirement works well for New York City. *Fordham Law Review, 76*, 1121–1191.

Fawcett, D. B. (1986). Eminent domain, the police power, and the Fifth Amendment: Defining the domain of the takings analysis. *University of Pittsburgh Law Review, 47*, 491–515.

Fee, J. (2006). Eminent domain and the sanctity of home. *Notre Dame Law Review, 81*, 783–819.

Fort Trumbull plan approved, but funding iffy. (2000, March 4). *The Day*. Retrieved March 10, 2011, from www.theday.com.

Foster, G. D. (1981). Law, morality, and the public servant. *Public Administration Review, 41*, 29–34.

Gallagher, E. F. (2005). Breaking new ground: Using eminent domain for economic development. *Fordham Law Review, 73*, 1837–1873.

Garnett, N. S. (2006). The neglected political economy of eminent domain. *Michigan Law Review, 105*, 101–150.

Garofalo, C. (2008). With deference to Woodrow Wilson: The ethics-administration dichotomy in American public service. *Public Integrity, 10*, 345–354.

Gaus, J. M. (1936). The responsibility of public administration. In J. M. Gaus, L. D. White, & M. E. Dimock (Eds.), *The frontiers of public administration* (pp. 26–44). Chicago, IL: University of Chicago Press.

Gooden, M. A. (2004). A history of black achievement as impacted by federal court decisions in the last century. *The Journal of Negro Education, 73*, 230–238.

Goodin, A. W. (2007). Rejecting the return to blight in post-*Kelo* state legislation. *New York University Law Review, 82*, 178–208.

Goodnow, F. J. (2003). *Politics and administration: A study in government.* New Brunswick, NJ: Transaction Publishers.

Goodsell, C. T. (1990). Public administration and the public interest. In G. L. Wamsley, R. N. Bacher, C. T. Goodsell, P. S. Kronenberg, J. A. Rohr, C. M. Stivers, O. F. White, & J. F. Wolf, *Refounding public administration* (pp. 96–113). Newbury Park, CA: Sage Publications, Inc.

———. (2004). *The case for bureaucracy: A public administration polemic* (4th ed.). Washington, DC: CQ Press.

Green, R. T. (1992). Constitutional jurisprudence: Reviving praxis in public administration. *Administration & Society, 24*, 3–21.

Green, R. T., Wamsley, G. L., & Keller, L. F. (1993). Reconstituting a profession for American public administration. *Public Administration Review, 53*, 516–524.

Han, A. S. (2008). From New London to Norwood: A year in the life of eminent domain. *Duke Law Journal, 57*, 1449–1483.

Haque, M. S. (2001). The diminishing publicness of public service under the current mode of governance. *Public Administration Review, 61*, 65–82.

Harrington, M. P. (2002). "Public use" and the original understanding of the so-called "Takings" Clause. *Hastings Law Journal, 53*, 1245.

Hart, D. K. (1984). The virtuous citizen, the honorable bureaucrat, and "public" administration. *Public Administration Review, 44*, 111–122.

Hawaii Housing Authority et al. v. Midkiff et al., 467 U.S. 229 (1984).

Hoyman, M. M. & McCall, J. R. (2010). Not imminent in my domain! County leaders' attitudes toward eminent domain decisions. *Public Administration Review, 70*, 885–893.

Hunter, R. C. (2004). The administration of court-ordered school desegregation in urban school districts: The law and experience. *The Journal of Negro Education, 73*, 218–229.

Kelly, D. B. (2006). The "public use" requirement in eminent domain law: A rationale based on secret purchases and private influences. *Cornell Law Review, 92*, 1–65.

Kelo et al. v. City of New London et al., 545 U.S. 469 (2005).

Knapp, G. S. (2008). Maintaining government accountability: Calls for a "public use" beyond eminent domain. *Indiana Law Journal, 83*, 1097–1119.

Lehavi, A. & Licht, A. N. (2007). Eminent domain, Inc. *Columbia Law Review, 107*, 1704–1748.

Lipsky, M. (1980). *Street–level bureaucracy: Dilemmas of individuals in public service.* New York, NY: Russel Sage.

Long, N. E. (1988). Public administration, cognitive competence, and the public interest. *Administration & Society, 20*, 334–343.

Lopez, E. J. & Totah, S. M. (2007). *Kelo* and its discontents: The worst (or best) thing to happen to property rights. *The Independent Review, 11*, 397–416.

Lynn, L. E., Jr. (1998). The new public management: How to transform a theme into a legacy. *Public Administration Review, 58*, 231–237.

———. (2001). The myth of the bureaucratic paradigm: What traditional public administration really stood for. *Public Administration Review, 61*, 144–160.

Lynn, L. E., Jr., Heinrich, C. J., & Hill, C. J. (2000). Studying governance and public management: Challenges and prospects. *Journal of Public Administration Research and Theory, 10*, 233–261.

Main, C. T. (2005). How eminent domain ran amok. *Policy Review, 133*, 3–24.

Mawdsley, R. D. (2000). *Missouri v. Jenkins*: Remaking an urban school district. *Education and Urban Society, 33*, 36–43.

Meier, K. J. (1997). Bureaucracy and democracy: The case for more bureaucracy and less democracy. *Public Administration Review, 57*, 193–199.

Melton, B. F., Jr. (1996). Eminent domain, "public use," and the conundrum of original intent. *Natural Resources Journal, 36*, 59–85.

Mihaly, M. B. (2007). Living in the past: The *Kelo* Court and public–private economic redevelopment. *Ecology Law Quarterly, 34*, 1–60.

Moe, R. C. (1994). The "reinventing government" exercise: Misinterpreting the problem, misjudging the consequences. *Public Administration Review, 54*, 111–122.

———. (2001). The emerging federal quasi government: Issues of management and accountability. *Public Administration Review, 61*, 290–312.

Morgan, D. F. (2001). The public interest. In T. L. Cooper (Ed.), *Handbook of administrative ethics* (2nd ed., pp. 151–178). New York: Marcel Dekker, Inc.

Mushkatel, A. & Nakhleh, K. (1978). Eminent domain: Land–use planning and the powerless in the United States and Israel. *Social Problems, 26*, 147–159.

Myers, B. L. (1977). Eminent domain: A legislative proposal for the reimbursement of condemnees' attorney's fees. *Indiana Law Journal, 52*, 813–835.

Neimann, P. & Shapiro, P. (2008). Efficiency and fairness: Compensation for takings. *International Review of Law and Economics, 28*, 157–165.

Odabashian, K. (2002). Investment–backed expectations and the politics of judicial articulation: The reintegration of history and the Lockean mind in contemporary American jurisprudence. *UCLA Law Review, 50*, 641–684.

Olejarski, A. M. (2011a). The *Kelo* opportunity: A loss for the Court, but a gain for public administrators. *Public Integrity, 13*, 41–58.

———. (2011b). Public good as public interest? The principle of tangibility in eminent domain legislation. *Public Integrity, 13*, 333–351.

Olejarski, A. M. & Webb Farley, K. (2013). The little blue pill that killed the little pink house: A narrative of eminent domain. *Administration & Society*, forthcoming.

O'Leary, R., David M. Van Slyke, & Soonhee Kim (Eds.). 2010. *The Future of Public Administration Around the World: The Minnowbrook Perspective*. Washington, DC: Georgetown University Press.

Perry, J. L. & Wise, L. R. (1990). The motivational bases of public service. *Public Administration Review, 50*, 367–373.

Perry, J. L. (1996). Measuring public service motivation: An assessment of construct reliability and validity. *Journal of Public Administration Research and Theory, 6*, 5–22.

———. (1997). Antecedents of public service motivation. *Journal of Public Administration Research and Theory, 7*, 181–197.

Petition seeking vote on demolition ruled invalid. (2000, October 3). *The Day*. Retrieved March 10, 2011, from www.theday.com

Pollock, P. H., III (2005). *The essentials of political analysis* (2nd ed.). Washington, DC: CQ Press.

Publius. (1961). *The Federalist*, J. E. Cook (Ed.). Cleveland, OH: Meridian Books.

Purchasing Power of Money in the United States from 1774 to Present. (n.d.). Retrieved March 29, 2011, from http://www.measuringworth.com/ppowerus/index.php

Riccucci, N. M. 2010. *Public Administration: Traditions of Inquiry and Philosophies of Knowledge*. Washington, DC: Georgetown University Press.

Rohr, J. A. (1989). *Ethics for bureaucrats: An essay on law and values* (2nd ed.) New York: Marcel Dekker, Inc.

Salkin, P. E. & Lucero, L. A. (2005). Community redevelopment, public use, and eminent domain. *The Urban Lawyer, 37*, 201–242.

Serkin, C. (2007). Local property law: Adjusting the scale of property protection. *Columbia Law Review, 107*, 883–948.

Simon, H. A. (1997). *Administrative behavior: A study of decision-making processes in administrative organizations* (4th ed.). New York, NY: The Free Press.

Spicer, M. W. & Terry, L. D. (1993). Legitimacy, history, and logic: Public administration and the Constitution. *Public Administration Review, 53*, 239–246.

Svara, J. H. (1985). Dichotomy and duality: Reconceptualizing the relationship between policy and administration in council–manager cities. *Public Administration Review, 45*, 221–232.

———. (1999a). Complementarity of politics and administration as a legitimate alternative to the dichotomy model. *Administration & Society, 30*, 676–705.

———. (1999b). The shifting boundary between elected officials and city managers in large council-manager cities. *Public Administration Review, 59*, 44–53.

———. (2001). The myth of the dichotomy: Complementarity of politics and administration in the past and future of public administration. *Public Administration Review, 61*, 176–183.

Town profiles. (n.d.). Retrieved July 10, 2009, from http://www.cerc.com/townprofiles/default.asp.

Waldo, D. (1952). Development of a theory of democratic administration. *The American Political Science Review, 46*, 81–103.

Wamsley, G. L., Goodsell, C. T., Rohr, J. A., Stivers, C. M., White, O. F., & Wolf, J. F. (1990). Public administration and the governance process: Shifting the political dialogue. In G. L. Wamsley, R. N. Bacher, C. T. Goodsell, P. S. Kronenberg, J. A. Rohr, C. M. Stivers, O. F. White, & J. F. Wolf, *Refounding public administration* (pp. 31–51). Newbury Park, CA: Sage Publications, Inc.

Wamsley, G. L. (1996). A public philosophy and ontological disclosure as the basis for normatively grounded theorizing in public administration. In G. L. Wamsley & J. Wolf (Eds.), *Refounding democratic public administration: Modern paradoxes, postmodern challenges* (pp. 351–401). Thousand Oaks, CA: Sage Publications, Inc.

Wilder, M. G. & Stigter, J. E. (1989). Rethinking the role of judicial scrutiny in eminent domain. *Journal of the American Planning Association, 55*, 57–65.

Wilson, W. (1887). The study of administration. *Political Science Quarterly, 2*, 197–222.

Zeiner, C. L. (2007). Establishing a leasehold through eminent domain: A slippery slope made treacherous by *Kelo*. *Catholic University Law Review, 56*, 503–55.

Index

Lightning Source UK Ltd.
Milton Keynes UK
UKHW03n0744200318
319731UK00009BA/227/P

9 780739 178584